2 BETTER ENGLISH EVERY DAY

Language for Living

PAUL J. HAMEL

Los Angeles Unified School District
Santa Monica College

HARCOURT BRACE & COMPANY
ORLANDO   SAN DIEGO   NEW YORK
TORONTO   LONDON   SYDNEY   TOKYO

LIBRARY OF CONGRESS CATALOGING IN PUBLICATION DATA

Main entry under title:

BETTER ENGLISH EVERYDAY 2 Language for Living
Includes appendices

1. English Language Textbook for foreigners   I. Hamel, Paul
PN6120.2.S89   1984   808.83'1   83-082148

ISBN 0-03-069603-8

Copyright © 1984 by IPS Publishing, Inc.

Requests for permission of any part of the work
should be mailed to: Permissions Department, Harcourt Brace &
Company, 8th Floor, Orlando, Florida 32887-6777.

    8 9 0 1 2 3 4 5 066 20 19 18 17 16 15 14 13

Address editorial correspondence to:
6277 Sea Harbor Drive
Orlando, Florida 62887-6777.

Printed in the United States of America

To the memory of my parents,
Wilfred and Yvonne Hamel

ACKNOWLEDGMENTS

Grateful acknowledgments are due to the many people who have encouraged me in writing this series. In particular I am indebted to Nancy Loncke for her invaluable contributions to this series in its early stages.

Special thanks to Elaine Kirn for her sound advice, for helping develop the format and for doing detailed editing. I would especially like to thank Tim Welch, Laura Welch, and Anne Boynton-Trigg for coordinating the production of the series; Pat Campbell, Nancy Cook, Linda Mrowicki, and Jean Zukowski/Faust for editing; Larry Layton for the book design; Frank Ridgeway and Betty Darwin for the art; Shelah Harris and Online Graphics for the typesetting; Becky Evans and Penny Yost for layout; and Bill Riling for lettering.

Special thanks also goes to the administrators, teachers, and students of Fairfax Community Adult School, Santa Monica City College, Jewish Vocational Service, and the Refugee Employment Training Project for their comments, suggestions, and assistance in developing the lessons.

I am especially grateful to David Chaille for his valuable ideas, insights, and for introducing me to publishing.

Last but not least, I am very grateful to George Gati for his editing, patience, understanding, and putting up with me during the many long hours it took to complete this series.

CONTENTS

INTRODUCTION
TO THE TEACHER

This series of three books is designed for adult students of English as a Second Language. It presents the grammar, vocabulary, and survival skills required in a basic ESL program. In addition, it supplies students with ample opportunity to practice the four language skills in the context of interesting and varied activities.

The major aim of this series is to present survival English so that newcomers can move more quickly into the labor market and function successfully on the job. The series covers critical survival skills needed to deal with real-life situations. The books emphasize finding and keeping a job, and the grammar program is highly integrated into prevocational materials and activities. Lessons carefully integrate survival skills, grammatical structures, and vocabulary to present practical and meaningful activities for the students. Grammatical structures are not presented and then forgotten. They reappear in multiple varied contexts throughout the series. The vocabulary, although often used in what appears to be nonvocational areas, represents common job-related words and are easily transferable to a work environment.

By the time students finish the series, they will have been exposed to enough English and job-related information to successfully begin work at an entry-level position or enter a technical English program.

TEACHING NOTES

These teaching notes detail some effective ways of teaching language skills. The basic techniques in these notes offer guidelines and suggestions to help the teacher present lessons in an effective and interesting way. We hope that these suggestions will inspire other, more creative techniques.

Listening Comprehension

The teacher may want to use the following techniques to develop effective listening comprehension skills.

1. After introducing key vocabulary words at the beginning of a reading lesson or dialog, slowly read the text aloud to your students before having them open their books. Then ask general comprehension questions. At the end of the reading lesson, dialog, or follow-up review exercise, read the text again at normal speed. The students should not be allowed to read along; they should concentrate on listening.
2. Give frequent short dictations. (See the section on dictation.)
3. When doing drills or question-and-answer exercises, have students cue one another whenever possible. This forces them to listen to each other and become accustomed to different accents.
4. Have students work in pairs and groups so that they can listen and respond to one another on a more personal level. (See the section on pairing and grouping.)
5. When practicing dialogs or role-playing, occasionally have pairs of students stand back-to-back so that they must understand each other without the aid of nonverbal cues.
6. Invite a guest speaker, the principal, the school nurse, a police officer, etc., to be interviewed in class so that the students can hear other accents and intonation. Before allowing the students to interview the speaker, prime the class by discussing the kinds of questions they will ask. By practicing the questions beforehand, students will be less embarrassed about asking questions or making mistakes.
7. Give the students the opportunity to listen to different examples of spoken English through music, games, movies, slide presentations, etc.

Dictation

Do not underestimate the usefulness of dictation. It can be a very effective tool for practicing the four language skills. It is especially useful as a warm-up exercise at the beginning of the class period to review previously covered materials. Frequent short dictations focusing on commonly used words and expressions used in simple sentences repeatedly stressing function words, such as articles, prepositions, pronouns, and auxiliary verbs, will do much to improve students' writing and spelling. Once students become accustomed to simple dictations presented in this series, you may want to vary the dictation format to keep interest high. As an example, try the following:

1. Dictate six questions.
2. After the students have written all six questions in their notebooks, have six volunteers write the questions on the chalkboard.
3. Have six other students read and correct the questions.
4. Have six more volunteers go up to the chalkboard and write the answers to the questions.
5. Have students read and correct the answers.
6. Discuss additional possible answers to the questions.

Other Suggestions:

1. Dictate the answers, and then have students write the questions.

2. Dictate single words that students must use in complete sentences.
3. Dictate jumbled sentences that students must put into correct word order.
4. Dictate sentences that students must change from affirmative to negative, interrogative to affirmative, etc.

Pronunciation, Spelling, and Word Building

Although teaching pronunciation and spelling should play a very important role in the beginning English class, it has too often been ignored. Despite many irregularly spelled words, some basic pronunciation and spelling rules can be taught early on to improve reading and writing skills. Keep such lessons short, introduce them frequently, and review them repeatedly.

Suggestions:

1. Use visuals, objects, pictures, and gestures as much as possible for constant reinforcement.
2. Do not overburden the students with too much pronunciation or spelling material at once. Do not teach more than one pronunciation lesson per day.
3. Irregularly spelled words should be taught separately from words that follow rules. A good way to teach them is through constant and frequent dictation.

Vocabulary

The following suggestions are only a few of those to be kept in mind when teaching vocabulary.

1. Use as many flash cards, objects (realia), and pictures as possible in order to reinforce the words visually. This will help hold interest and aid students in remembering new vocabulary.
2. Define the words and give many contextual examples in sentences, expressions, and situations. Also help define and contrast the new vocabulary with synonyms, antonyms, and homonyms.
3. When selecting vocabulary, concentrate on practical, high frequency, functional vocabulary and expressions.
4. Do not overburden your students with too many vocabulary items at any one time. Introduce ten or so new words per lesson.

Suggested Activities:

1. Flash Cards: Write new words on 5" x 8" index cards and use them in your lessons. Daily add a few new words. Mix them up and use them for review. Continually add to them until you have developed a valuable word bank. Use the cards for pronunciation practice, drills, recognition (i.e., have students make complete sentences with the words), dictation, spelling bees, and other word games.

2. Conversation Practice: Cut out pictures describing *every day* life from newspapers and magazines and paste them on construction paper. Then, on the back of each picture, write four or five vocabulary words represented in the picture (a noun, a verb, an adjective, and a preposition). Even if many more words could be added, limit the number. Divide the class into pairs or small groups and distribute the pictures. (See the section on pairing and grouping.) Tell the students to use the vocabulary on the back of the pictures to identify the objects and discuss what is happening. As a variation, write a list of question words on the chalkboard and have students use them in asking one another questions. Walk around the classroom, listening, and correcting errors and spending time with the weaker students. Let groups exchange pictures to continue the exercise.

3. Tic-tac-toe: Draw a tic-tac-toe grid and fill it in with vocabulary. Divide the class into two teams, each team assigned the symbol "X" or "O." Then flip a coin to determine which team begins. Have the students take turns in an orderly fashion by going down the rows. Tell the first student of the first team to use any word from the grid in a sentence. If the sentence is correct, replace the word with the team's symbol, X or O. Otherwise, leave the word. Go on to the first person on the other team. Continue in this manner until one team wins by having three consecutive X's or O's in a row vertically, horizontally, or diagonally. Keep score by giving one point for each game won. After each game, replace all the words in the grid with a different category of words such as all prepositions, all verbs, all antonym pairs, etc.

4. Crossword Puzzle: Draw a grid and words on the chalkboard. Divide the class into two teams and flip a coin to determine which team goes first. Have the first student of the first team go to the chalkboard and write a word that uses one letter of an existing word in the crossword. If the word fits and is correctly spelled, give one point for every letter of the new word. Then, go on to the first student of the other team. If the word is incorrect, erase it and go to the opposite team.

Pair Practice and Grouping

Pairing and grouping exercises give the students time, especially in large classes, to practice important speaking skills. Organizing students to work together can be somewhat frustrating at the start, but once they clearly understand what you expect of them, subsequent pairing or grouping activities usually proceed smoothly. Most pair practice exercises consist of simple substitution or transformation drills that you can also use for drilling the class as a whole.

Pair Practice:

1. Explain that this kind of exercise is to allow students to practice their *speaking* skills, not their writing skills. Tell students to put away all writing materials.
2. Have each student choose a partner. You will probably have to go around the classroom and pair students up the first few times you do this type of activity. Encourage students to pair up with different partners each time.
3. Indicate the material you want the students to practice.
4. Walk around the classroom, listening to individual students and correcting any errors that you hear. This provides an excellent opportunity to spend time with your weaker students.

Grouping:

In more advanced classes, dividing students into small groups for conversation practice is especially effective.

1. Divide the class into groups of four or five.
2. Present a problem, values clarification, for example, and tell the students that they must come up with a solution to the problem that all members of the group support unanimously.
3. While the groups are discussing, compromising, and agreeing on solutions, walk around the classroom to answer questions or correct any mistakes you hear.
4. Bring the whole class together for a general discussion to compare the various answers.

Reading

Some suggestions:

1. Before reading the dialog or passage, introduce the new vocabulary and grammatical structures. For effective visual reinforcement, use the chalkboard, flash cards, and pictures. Give many contextual examples of new words.
2. Read the text. The students should not see the text at this point. Use this time as a listening comprehension exercise. (See the section on listening comprehension.)
3. Ask general comprehension questions.
4. Read the text a second time, with the students reading along. As you read, tell the students to underline any unfamiliar vocabulary and expressions.
5. Discuss the vocabulary and expressions the students have underlined.
6. Ask more detailed comprehension questions.
7. Have volunteers read the passage aloud. (optional)

Other Suggestions:

1. Have students read the text silently. Then ask basic comprehension questions.
2. Have students retell the story in their own words.
3. After asking detailed comprehension questions, have students ask their own detailed questions of each other.
4. On another day, give a short dictation based on part of the text. (See section on dictation.)
5. Prepare a handout of the text with some of the vocabulary items missing (cloze-type exercise). Have students supply the words.
6. Have students write a story modeled on the text or dialog.
7. If possible, have students change the story from dialog to text or vise versa.
8. Do a read-and-look-up exercise: have students read a sentence silently, then try to repeat as much of the sentence as they can without looking at the book.
9. Prepare a handout of a text or dialog with some of the words missing. Read the text aloud and have students fill in the missing words as they read along.

Dialogs

Some suggestions:

1. Before presenting the dialog to the class, select and introduce any vocabulary items and structures that the students are not familiar with.
2. Read the dialog once for general comprehension. You may want to let the students read along.
3. Have students close their books.
4. Read the first line aloud, and then have the students repeat it. If necessary, have them repeat it several times for correct pronunciation and intonation.
5. Teach the second line (rejoinder) in the same manner. If the line is too long, present it in segments.
6. Repeat the first line, having a student respond with the rejoinder. Then reverse roles.
7. Select two students to repeat the two lines.
8. Teach the next two lines in the same manner.
9. Return to the beginning of the dialog and review it to the point where you left off.
10. Continue to the end of the dialog. (If the dialog is very long, select only one part. Do not try to teach dialogs which are more than eight or ten lines.)

Other Suggestions:

1. Write the first part of the rejoinder on the chalkboard and have students come up to write the second part.
2. Give part of the dialog as a dictation on a subsequent day.
3. As a written quiz, prepare a handout of the dialog with some of the key vocabulary items missing. Have students fill in the blanks from memory.

4. Have students write their own dialog modeled on the text.
5. Have students rewrite the dialog as a narrative.
6. Adapt the dialog to be used as the basis of a role-playing exercise. (See the section on role-playing.)

Writing

Expose students through short frequent exercises to writing that is closely related to the vocabulary, structures, and topics you have already taught. Exercises should also be varied, practical, and related to students' daily lives.

Be careful not to overwhelm students. Begin this program with simple exercises such as addressing envelopes and writing postcards, notes, and shopping lists. Such initial practice will give students time to learn the most commonly used words, which are also the most irregularly spelled, such as pronouns, articles, prepositions, and auxiliary verbs. Once students have learned the basics, gradually build up to longer and more complex exercises.

Other Suggestions:

1. Assign writing exercises that reinforce or review previously learned material.
2. When giving a writing assignment as homework, reserve the last part of the class period for writing. This will allow you to walk around the classroom to make sure everyone understands the assignment.
3. When correcting the students' papers, correct only serious mistakes in structure and spelling. Praise the correct use of recently taught vocabulary and structures.
4. If you find mistakes that several students are making, note them and teach a special lesson based on these mistakes.
5. Include the entire class in the correcting process by copying the incorrect sentences taken from their papers onto the chalkboard or on a handout. Have a class discussion on how best to correct the mistakes.
6. Have students rewrite their corrected exercises in their notebooks.
7. Keep a list of spelling errors to be used in a future dictation.

Grammar

Some Suggestions:

1. Present grammar sequenced in order of increasing difficulty. For example, introduce the simple past tense before teaching the present perfect. With major grammatical structures, such as the use of the simple past, introduce structures in well-spaced segments. Don't try to teach all the irregular verbs at once. It is more appropriate to teach a few at a time over a long period.

2. In introducing grammar, use situations, visuals, and graphics to give students several different ways of understanding the structure.
3. Present and reinforce grammar in the context of survival skills, situations, activities, stories, and games. For example, when teaching the possessive *of,* also teach the names of food containers (carton *of* milk, can *of* soup, etc.).
4. End all lessons, or do follow-up reviews, with communicative activities, such as role-playing, incorporating the grammatical structure. For example, after teaching *some* and *any,* role-play ordering food in a restaurant. For teaching prepositions, set up an obstacle course in the classroom and have students direct each other through it. (See the section on role-playing.)
5. When presenting drills, vary them whenever possible. Cue responses with gestures, objects, pictures, and flash cards.
6. In nonacademic courses, minimize the use of grammatical terms. For instance, most students are interested in learning how to *use* the structures rather than in knowing the differences between transitive and intransitive verbs.
7. Constantly review previously taught grammar. Reintroduce it in another context, contrast it with another grammatical structure, or build it into another lesson.

Role-Playing

Use role-playing to expand your lessons and reinforce vocabulary and structures. Before expecting students to perform successfully in role-playing exercises, consider the following:

1. Discuss the situation beforehand so that students can familiarize themselves with the topic as well as with necessary vocabulary and structure.
2. Teach a dialog as a primer, or allow students to prepare themselves in pairs or small groups. (See the section on pair practice.)
3. Have students do each role-playing exercise twice, the first time with teacher participation and the second time without.
4. Encourage students to vary situations and be creative.
5. Don't over-correct. Note major mistakes; discuss and correct them later. To practice active listening, have the class note errors, too.
6. Discuss the role-playing exercise afterward for students' reaction and interpretations.

Some Basic Situations:

Asking and giving street directions; looking at and asking questions about a new apartment; calling the telephone operator for information; buying an item in a store; going on a job interview; speaking to a doctor, dentist, or pharmacist; getting a driver's license; introducing and meeting people at a party; making or canceling an appointment; leaving a message; asking a postal clerk about correct postage; cashing a check; opening a checking or savings account at a bank; ordering food at a restaurant; etc.

General Suggestions

1. Create an atmosphere where students are not afraid to make mistakes. Simple communication is more important than speaking perfectly.
2. Encourage students to use what they have learned in class in their speech. Encourage them to speak to one another in English during their breaks and free time. You might even reserve a special "English table" or area in your classroom where students can practice while having a snack or a cup of coffee.
3. Be eclectic. Use any method, technique, or combination of methods that work for you and your students.
4. Use as much variety in your lessons as possible.
5. Space your best lessons and activities throughout the course to keep interest high. Don't empty your entire "bag of tricks" early on.
6. Make and collect as many teaching aids (visuals, objects, handouts) as possible. Store them for future use.
7. Require that your students bring dictionaries to school and use them often.

1

WELCOME BACK; REVIEW OF BOOK ONE

COMPETENCIES	• **Introducing People** • **Asking and Giving Directions** • **Reading a Shopping Directory, Schedule of Classes, and Bus Schedule** • **Filling Out a School Registration Form** • **Filling Out a Job Application** • **Responding to Interview Questions**
GRAMMAR	• **The Simple Present Tense** • **The Present Continuous Tense** • *can, may* • **Subject and Object Pronouns** • **Possessive Adjectives**
VOCABULARY	• **Basic School, Bus, Shopping, and Job Search Vocabulary**

LISTEN

Miko Takahashi and Sami Hamati meet after the semester break.

Miko: Hi, Sami.
Sami: Hi, Miko.
Miko: Well, here we are again.
Sami: What class are you in this semester?
Miko: In ESL 2. What about you?
Sami: I'm in ESL 2, too.
Miko: What classroom are you in?
Sami: Room 204.
Miko: So am I. Who's our teacher?
Sami: Mr. Barns, I think.
Miko: Doesn't he teach Level One?
Sami: This semester he's teaching Level Two.
Miko: Great! He's a really good teacher.

UNDERSTAND   *Circle True, False, or We don't know.*

1. It's a new semester.	(True)	False	We don't know.
2. Sami and Miko are both in the same class.	True	False	We don't know.
3. It's January.	True	False	We don't know.
4. Miko likes Mr. Barns.	True	False	We don't know.
5. "So am I" means "Me, too."	True	False	We don't know.
6. "ESL" means "English as a Second Language."	True	False	We don't know.

READ

SCHEDULE OF CLASSES

Directory

| Principal | 101 | | | Main Office | 103 |
| Vice Principal | 102 | | | Counselor | 104 |

CLASS	LEVEL	ROOM	TIME	DAYS	TEACHER
Typing	1	109*	6:30-9:30 p.m.	M & W**	Mr. Brown
Typing	2	110	6:30-9:30	T & Th	Mr. Brown
Wood Shop	1-2	206	6:30-9:30	M & W	Mr. Fuller
Auto Mechanics	1	207	6:30-9:30	T & Th	Ms. Kirn
ESL	1	123	2:30-5:00	M - Th***	Mrs. Rose
ESL	1	204	7:00-9:30	M - Th	Ms. Childs
ESL	2	315	7:00-9:30	M - Th	Mr. Barns
ESL	2	210	7:00-9:30	M - Th	Miss Sumner
ESL	3	303	7:00-9:30	M - Th	Mr. Thompson

PAIR PRACTICE   *Talk with another student about the schedule above.*

Student 1: What room is .... (class) in?
                      or
              What floor is .... (class) on?
                      or
              What time does .... begin?
                      or
              What days does .... meet?
                      or
              Who's the .... teacher?
Student 2: ....

---

*   The first number of the room number tells the floor. Example: Room **2**03 is on the second floor.

**   & = and. (M & W means two days a week, Monday and Wednesday.)

***   – = through. (M – Th means four times a week, Monday, Tuesday, Wednesday, and Thursday.)

LISTEN

Maria and her friend, Carmen Martinez, join Sami and Miko.

Maria:	Hi, Sami. Hi, Miko.
	I want you to meet a friend.
	This is Carmen Martinez. She's from Colombia.
	Carmen, these are my friends, Sami and Miko.
Carmen:	Pleased to meet you.
Miko and Sami:	Pleased to meet you, too.
Maria:	Here comes David Fernandez.
David:	Hi, everybody.
Maria:	Do you know Carmen?
David:	No, I don't.
Carmen:	Hello. My name's Carmen Martinez.
David:	I'm David Fernandez.
Carmen:	Glad to meet you.
David:	Glad to meet you, too.

PAIR PRACTICE   *Walk around the classroom and practice the dialog below with other students.*

Student 1:	Hello, I'm ....
Student 2:	Hi, I'm ....
Student 1:	Pleased to meet you.
Student 2:	Pleased to meet you, too.

PAIR PRACTICE   *Walk around the classroom and introduce one student to another.*

Student 1:	This is ....
	He's/She's from ....
Student 2:	Glad to meet you.
Student 3:	Glad to meet you, too.

READ

Carmen registers for a class.

Sami: This is a new student. She wants to register for an ESL class.
Counselor: What level?
Carmen: Level Three.
Counselor: Please fill out this registration card.

WRITE *Help Carmen fill out her registration card.*

I'M CARMEN MARTINEZ. MY MIDDLE NAME IS MARIA. I'M FROM COLOMBIA. I WANT TO STUDY ENGLISH. I WANT TO BE IN A LEVEL THREE ESL CLASS. I PASSED A PLACEMENT TEST FOR LEVEL THREE. I LIVE AT 39 OCEAN STREET, SANTA MONICA, CALIFORNIA. MY ZIP CODE IS NINE-TWO-OH-SIX-NINE. MY TELEPHONE NUMBER IS THREE-FOUR-TWO-SIX-ZERO-SEVEN-NINE. I'M NINETEEN YEARS OLD. MY BIRTHDAY IS NOVEMBER SIXTH.

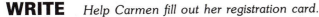

```
                    REGISTRATION CARD


NAME: _____
           Last       First        Middle

ADDRESS: _____
              Number       Street       Apartment

CITY: _____ STATE: ____ ZIP CODE: _____

DATE OF BIRTH: _____ NATIONALITY: _____

CLASS: _____ LEVEL: _____

TELEPHONE: _____ SIGNATURE: _____
```

Abbreviations:

St. = street
Ave. = avenue
Blvd. = boulevard
Dr. = drive
Rd. = road
Apt. = apartment
# = number
N. = north
S. = south
E. = east
W. = west

UNDERSTAND *Circle **True**, **False**, or **We don't know**.*

1. Sami's a new student.	True	False	We don't know.
2. Carmen lives in an apartment.	True	False	We don't know.
3. Carmen's year of birth is 1965.	True	False	We don't know.
4. Carmen's telephone number is 342-6079.	True	False	We don't know.

READ

Sami, Maria, and Carmen go to the snack bar across the street.

WE HAVE A FEW MINUTES BEFORE OUR CLASSES. LET'S GO TO THE SNACK BAR ACROSS THE STREET AND MEET MARIO.

O.K.

ALL RIGHT.

Sami, Maria, and Carmen are standing at the door of the snack bar.

LOOK! THERE ARE RAYMOND AND ROBERTO MONTE. THEY'RE TWINS.
RAYMOND LIVES IN LOS ANGELES.
ROBERTO LIVES IN SANTA MONICA.
RAYMOND RENTS A HOUSE.
ROBERTO RENTS AN APARTMENT.
RAYMOND WORKS FOR A TRUCKING COMPANY.
ROBERTO WORKS IN AN OFFICE.

SNACK BAR

WHAT? CAN YOU REPEAT THAT?

WRITE   *Help Maria describe Raymond and Roberto Monte. Fill in the spaces with present tense verbs. Use the **-s** ending, and the negative with **doesn't**. (Remember that she is talking about regular or habitual actions.)*

1. Raymond *lives* in Los Angeles; he *doesn't live* in Santa Monica.

2. Raymond _____ a house; he _____ _____ an apartment.

3. Raymond _____ for a trucking company; he _____ _____ in an office.

WRITE   *Fill in the spaces with **does** or **doesn't**.*

1. *Does* Raymond rent a house?

2. _____ Roberto live in Los Angeles?

3. _____ Raymond work for a trucking company?

4. _____ Roberto drive a truck?

5. _____ Roberto live in an apartment?

Of course, he *does* .

No, he _____ .

Sure he _____ .

No, he _____ .

He sure _____ .

READ

Sami sees some of his friends.

AND THERE ARE WANDA AND STEPHEN BRATKO.
AND LI AND YEN CHU.
WANDA AND STEPHEN COME FROM POLAND.
LI AND YEN COME FROM HONG KONG.
WANDA AND STEPHEN HAVE TWO KIDS.
LI AND YEN HAVE ONE CHILD.
WANDA AND STEPHEN LIVE NEAR HERE.
LI AND YEN LIVE FAR AWAY.
WANDA AND STEPHEN WALK TO SCHOOL.
LI AND YEN DRIVE HERE.

WHAT? PLEASE REPEAT THAT!

SNACK BAR

WRITE   *Fill in the spaces with present tense verbs. Use **don't** in the negative.*

1. Li and Yen Chu _____ from Hong Kong; they _____ _____ from Poland.

2. Li and Yen _____ only one child; they _____ _____ two kids.

3. Li and Yen _____ far from school; they _____ _____ near school.

4. Li and Yen _____ a car to school; they _____ _____ to school.

SNACK BAR

WRITE   *Fill in the spaces with the correct verb and **do, does, don't**, or **doesn't**.*

1. *Does* ____ Wanda *come* ____ from Poland?   Yes, she *does* ____.

2. _____ Li and Yen _____ from Poland, too?   No, they _____.

3. _____ Wanda _____ two kids?   Uh-huh, she_____.

4. _____ Li and Yen _____ near school?   No, they _____.

5. _____ Wanda and Stephen _____ near school?   They sure_____.

6. _____ Li _____ a car to school?   Sure he _____.

WRITE
Fill in the spaces with the correct present continuous form of the verb under the lines. (Remember that they are talking about continuous action in the present time.)

Sami, Maria, and Carmen go to Mario's table at the snack bar. Mario is sitting with a friend, Peter Boulos.

Sami: Hi, Mario. Hi, Peter.

Maria: How are you?

Peter: Fine. How _____are_____ you _____doing_____?
                                    (1) do

Sami: I _____ _____ fine. What _____ you _____?
                    (2) do   (3) do

Mario: We _____ _____ before class. I _____ _____ a cup of
                      (4) rest   (5) have

coffee, and Peter _____ _____ dinner.
                          (6) eat

Maria: There are a lot of students here.

Peter: And the waitress is really busy. She _____ _____ from table to table. Look!
                                                        (7) run

The manager _____ _____ her, too. They _____ _____
                    (8) help   (9) try

to serve all of us before the classes begin.

Maria: Peter, where's your wife?

Peter: She _____ _____ over there near the window. She
                  (10) stand

_____ _____ to Tan and Lan Tran. She _____ _____ them
      (11) talk   (12) tell

about our new apartment.

Waitress: May I help you?

Carmen: No, thank you. We _____ _____ now. We don't want to be late for class.
                                (13) leave

Peter: I'll leave the tip.

GROUP DISCUSSION
Talk about restaurant etiquette and tipping.

READ

Maria, Mario, Carmen, and Sami are walking in the hall.

WHAT ROOM IS THAT?

IT'S THE TEACHERS' ROOM.

WRITE   *Fill in the spaces below with the words in the box.*

Subject Pronouns:	I	you	he	she	it	we	they
Possessive Adjectives:	my	your	his	her	its	our	their
Object Pronouns:	me	you	him	her	it	us	them

That's Mr. Thompson. ___*He*___'s your teacher. ___*His*___ first name's Percy. The students like ___*him*___ very much.

There's Ms. Sumner. _____'s a teacher and an actress. _____ classroom is next door. Mr. Thompson is speaking to _____ now.

There's Mr. Barns. _____ is my teacher. _____'s an excellent teacher. _____ lessons are very interesting. I learn a lot from _____.

Mr. Barns, Mario, and I sometimes take a break together. _____ go to the catering truck downstairs. _____ friends sometimes join _____, too.

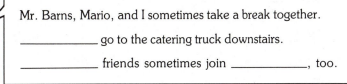

WRITE   *Fill in the spaces with the simple present or present continuous form of the verb under the line.*

The students are waiting for their teachers in front of the classrooms.

Where's Lisa?

She*'s working* now.
work

Oh? Where *does* she *work* ?
work

She *works* at the hospital on
work

Monday and Tuesday.

Does she *like* her job?
like

Yes, she *does* .
do

What _____ he _____?
do

He _____ _____ a pen.
look for

Why _____ he _____ a pen?
need

He _____ to write a note to his girlfriend.
want

What _____ you _____?
read

I _____ a book about American history.
read

_____ you _____ history books?
like

Yes, I _____. What about you?
do

I _____ love stories.
like

Why _____ you _____ here?
wait

We _____ _____ for our teacher.
wait

_____ you _____ to school early
come

every day?

Yes, we _____.
do

Why?

Because we _____ good seats.
want

READ

Carmen is speaking to Wanda.

Wanda: Where do you work?
Carmen: I don't have a job. I'm looking for one now.
Wanda: What kind of work do you do?
Carmen: I'm an electronics assembler.
Wanda: Try the Byte Computer Company on Fifth Street.
Carmen: How can I get there? I don't have a car.
Wanda: Take the #93 bus. You can catch it on First Street in front of the school.
Carmen: What time does it stop there?
Wanda: Here's a bus schedule. You can keep it.
Carmen: Thanks a lot for your help.

PAIR PRACTICE   *Talk with another student about the bus schedule below.*

Student 1: When does the bus stop at .... and ....?
Student 2: It stops there at ....

WHEN DOES THE BUS STOP AT FIRST AND MAIN?

IT STOPS THERE AT NINETEEN PAST THREE, TWENTY TO FOUR,....

BUS SCHEDULE		LINE 93		
INBOUND TO DOWNTOWN				
Fifth St. & Main St.	Fourth St. & Main St.	Third St. & Main St.	Second St. & Main St.	First St. & Main St.
2:44 p.m.	2:59	3:04	3:11	3:19
3:05	3:20	3:25	3:32	3:40
3:29	3:44	3:49	3:56	4:04
4:29	4:44	4:49	4:56	5:04
5:00	5:15	5:20	5:27	5:35
5:22	5:37	5:42	5:49	5:57
5:50	6:05	6:10	6:17	6:25
6:21	6:36	6:40	6:47	6:55

READ

An hour later, during the break, Carmen is talking to Maria.

Carmen: Maria, can you go with me tomorrow? I want to apply for a job at a computer company on Fifth Street.

  Maria: I'm sorry, but I can't. I work, you know.

Carmen: Oh, right. Before I go, I need to get a new dress, some shoes, and a haircut. Where can I get all that?

  Maria: At the Lincoln Shopping Center. There's a computer store in the shopping center, and the computer company is next door to it.

UNDERSTAND   *Circle **True**, **False**, or **We don't know**.*

1. Maria and Carmen are at a shopping center.   True   False   We don't know.
2. Maria can go with Carmen.   True   False   We don't know.

LINCOLN SHOPPING CENTER DIRECTORY

	Floor		Floor		Floor
Information Desk	1	Radio and T.V. Store	5	Stationery Store	4
Hairdresser	3	Department Store	1	Business Offices	5
Barber	3	Movie Theaters	4	Lost and Found	1
Restaurants	5	Pet Shop	5	Security Office	1
Coffee Shop	2	Men's Clothing	3	Shoe Store	2
Bookstore	4	Women's Clothing	4	Byte Computer Store	5
Drugstore	1	Children's Clothing	3	Restrooms	1
Toy Store	5	Hardware Store	2		

PAIR PRACTICE   *Talk with another student about the items below. Use the directory above.*

Student 1: Where can I get ....?
Student 2: You can get .... at the ....

1.   2.   3.   4.

5.   6.   7.   8.

PAIR PRACTICE   *Use the directory above.*

Student 1: What floor is the .... on?
Student 2: It's on the .... floor.

CHALLENGE   *Alphabetize the directory above.*

READ

Carmen is applying for a job at the Byte Computer Company.

Carmen: Is this the Personnel Office?
Receptionist: Yes, it is. May I help you?
Carmen: I want to apply for a job.
Receptionist: Please fill out this application and wait here.

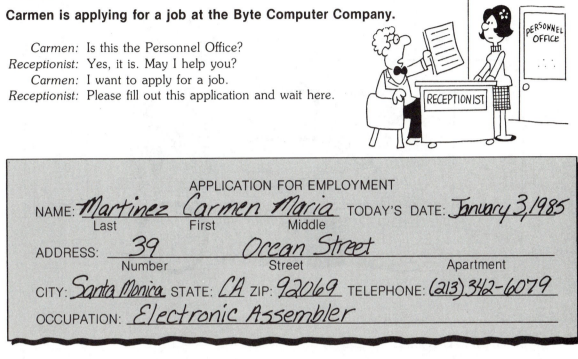

APPLICATION FOR EMPLOYMENT

NAME: *Martinez   Carmen   Maria*   TODAY'S DATE: *January 3, 1985*
　　　　　Last　　　　First　　　　Middle

ADDRESS: ___*39*___ ___*Ocean Street*___
　　　　　Number　　　　　Street　　　　　　　Apartment

CITY: *Santa Monica* STATE: *CA* ZIP: *92069* TELEPHONE: *(213) 342-6079*

OCCUPATION: *Electronic Assembler*

WRITE   *Now you fill out an application for a job.*

APPLICATION FOR EMPLOYMENT

NAME: _____ TODAY'S DATE: _____
　　　　　Last　　　　First　　　　Middle

ADDRESS: _____
　　　　　Number　　　　　Street　　　　　　Apartment

CITY: _____ STATE: ___ ZIP: _____ TELEPHONE: _____

OCCUPATION: _____

When can you begin to work? _____

Can you work on weekends? _____

Can you work at night? _____

Your last job: Where? _____ When? _____

Do you have a job now? _____

SIGNATURE: _____

WRITE   *Fill in the spaces below with the words in the box.*

'm	is	's	are	do	don't	can

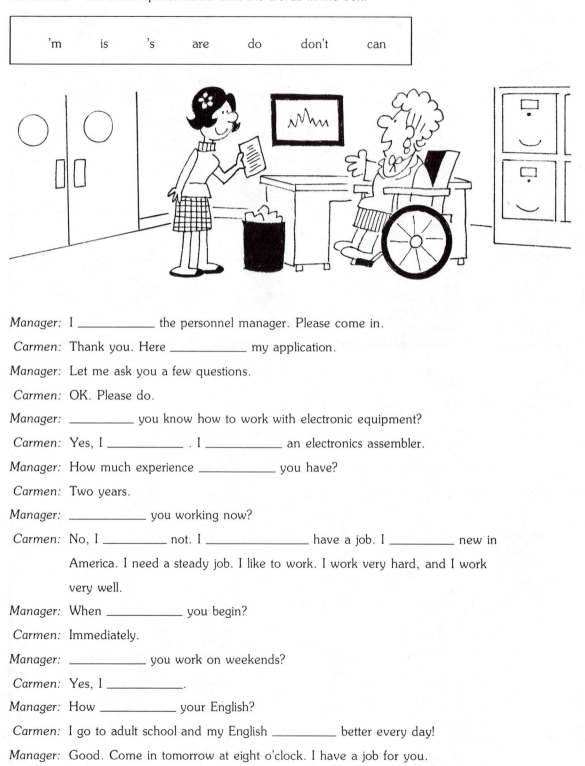

Manager: I _____ the personnel manager. Please come in.

Carmen: Thank you. Here _____ my application.

Manager: Let me ask you a few questions.

Carmen: OK. Please do.

Manager: _____ you know how to work with electronic equipment?

Carmen: Yes, I _____ . I _____ an electronics assembler.

Manager: How much experience _____ you have?

Carmen: Two years.

Manager: _____ you working now?

Carmen: No, I _____ not. I _____ have a job. I _____ new in
America. I need a steady job. I like to work. I work very hard, and I work
very well.

Manager: When _____ you begin?

Carmen: Immediately.

Manager: _____ you work on weekends?

Carmen: Yes, I _____ .

Manager: How _____ your English?

Carmen: I go to adult school and my English _____ better every day!

Manager: Good. Come in tomorrow at eight o'clock. I have a job for you.

PAIR PRACTICE   *Fold the page down the middle. Look only at your side. Follow the instructions.*

Student 1

Listen to the questions from your partner and find the answers in the Schedule of Classes below.

```
SCHEDULE OF CLASSES
   Afternoon Classes

CLASS      ROOM   TIME    TEACHER

ESL 1       123   2:30     Mr. West
ESL 2       124   2:30     Mrs. Wood
ESL 3       127   5:00     Ms. Gold
French 1    214   3:30     Mrs. Green
Spanish 1   213   4:00     Mr. Ruiz
Typing      322   3:00     Mr. Gee
```

Your partner fills out an identification card for you. Tell your partner your:

1. first name,

2. last name,

3. address,

4. city,

5. state,

6. zip code,

7. telephone number,

8. date of birth,

9. nationality,

10. class,

11. and level.

Student 2

Ask your partner these questions.

1. What room is the French class in?

2. What floor is the typing class on?

3. Who's the ESL 3 teacher?

4. What time does the Spanish class begin?

5. What room is ESL 1 in?

6. What floor is the Spanish class on?

7. What time does ESL 2 begin?

8. Who's Mr. Gee?

Fill in the identification card for your partner. Listen to the information.

```
IDENTIFICATION CARD

NAME: _____

ADDRESS: _____

CITY: _____

STATE: _____ ZIP: _____

TELEPHONE: _____

DATE OF BIRTH: _____

NATIONALITY: _____

CLASS: _____ LEVEL: _____

SIGNATURE: _____
```

FOLD HERE

GROUP ACTIVITY
Walk around the classroom, look at your classmates, and ask questions. Find the students with the following characteristic(s). Then write their names in the spaces below.

1. _____
   has a job.

2. _____
   doesn't work.

3. _____
   lives near school.

4. _____
   lives far from school.

5. _____
   is wearing a white shirt.

6. _____
   is wearing a red blouse.

7. _____
   is handsome.

8. _____
   is pretty.

9. _____
   has one brother and a sister.

10. _____
   has a car.

11. _____
   takes the bus to school.

12. _____
   can speak my language.

WRITE
Find as many words as you can. Write the words below.

```
m a n y e s p r a c t i c e s
n i n e a r e a n o t s i u i
w m a n t b i g s a y u r e t
c a t o o l m d a t e n u s e
e p i c t u r e d h s d c p a
n o t t h e e s e a t a k e s
t s i z r m s k n t r y m a y
h s t r e e t i m e n m a k e
i o f r e e x r i g h t a p e
s a b o u t z t w e i v e i l
```

man

nine

wait

cat

eat

_____

2

IT'S TOO WET TO WALK HOME

COMPETENCIES	• Understanding a Weather Forecast
	• Reading a Weather Forecast
	• Using Fahrenheit and Centigrade Thermometers
GRAMMAR	• Adverbs of Frequency
	• *to be* + Adjective + Infinitive
	• *too/enough*
VOCABULARY	• Frequency Words
	• Weather/Temperature
	• Common Adjectives
	• Basic Job Vocabulary
WORD BUILDING	• Changing Nouns to Adjectives with the Suffix *-y*
	• Negative Prefixes

LISTEN

The personnel manager introduces Carmen to Vic Pontrelli, her new supervisor at work.

Vic: Here's your badge, Carmen. You must always wear it at work. We usually work eight hours a day, and we sometimes work only half a day before holidays. We never work on legal holidays. We punch in at 8:00 a.m. and we punch out at 5:00 p.m. Sometimes we work overtime, but only two or three times a month.

Manager: We take fifteen-minute breaks twice a day, midmorning and midafternoon. We seldom take our breaks before 10:00 a.m. or after 4:00 p.m.

Carmen: How many times a month do we get a paycheck?

Vic: Twice a month, and we generally get a raise once a year.

UNDERSTAND   *Circle **True**, **False**, or **We don't know**.*

1. "Not often" means "seldom."	True	False	We don't know.
2. The employees work eight hours a day.	True	False	We don't know.
3. The employer pays the workers for holidays.	True	False	We don't know.
4. Lunch is one hour.	True	False	We don't know.
5. A "raise" means "more money."	True	False	We don't know.
6. "Overtime" means "extra time."	True	False	We don't know.

GRAMMAR   Adverbs of Frequency

- *Adverbs of frequency tell how often an action happens. The percentages below show approximately what frequency of occurrence each word represents.*

always – 100%	sometimes – 50%
generally, usually – 90%	seldom – 20%
often – 75%	never – 0%

- *Adverbs of frequency come before the main verb of a sentence.*

EXAMPLES

We	**usually**	work eight hours.
We	**sometimes**	work half a day.
We	**never**	work on holidays.
We	**seldom**	take breaks before 10 a.m.
We	**generally**	get a raise every year.

But they follow the verb **be** *and modal verbs.*

EXAMPLES

It isn't	**often.**	
You must	**always**	wear the badge at work.

- *Adverbs of frequency can appear at the beginning of a sentence.*

EXAMPLE   **Sometimes**   we work overtime.

- *We often use the adverb* **ever** *in questions. We never use* **ever** *in positive sentences.*

EXAMPLE   Do you   **ever**   work overtime?

READ   *Make logical complete sentences with the words in the box.*

	always	take a break	on time.
	generally	work	early.
I	usually	work overtime	late.
Employees	often	get a raise	eight hours.
We	sometimes	go home	every day.
They	seldom	come to work	every month.
	never	arrive at school	every year.

PAIR PRACTICE   *Talk with another student. Use adverbs of frequency with the phrases below.*

Student 1: How often do/are you ....?
Student 2: I ....

1. work overtime
2. be sick
3. come to school late
4. come to school early
5. be on time
6. get a paycheck
7. sleep late
8. get a letter
9. ask questions
10. speak English
11. read the newspaper
12. work on the weekend

HOW OFTEN DO YOU WORK OVERTIME?

I SELDOM WORK OVERTIME.

GRAMMAR　Adverbial Expressions of Time

> • *Long adverbial expressions of time generally come at the end of the sentence.*
>
> | *EXAMPLES* | We | work | **eight hours a day.** |
> | --- | --- | --- | --- |
> | | We | work overtime | **two or three times a month.** |
> | | We | take a break | **twice a day.** |
> | | We | get a raise | **once a year.** |

READ　*Make logical complete sentences with the words in the box.*

	take a bus	once	
I	get a paycheck	twice	a day.*
We	work overtime	three times	a week.
Employees	work	four times	a month.
They	get a raise	five times	a year.
	come to work early	eight hours	

PAIR PRACTICE　*Talk with another student. Use adverbial expressions of time with the phrases below.*

Student 1: How often do you ....?
Student 2: I ....

1. work overtime
2. see your parents
3. see your relatives
4. come home late from work (or school)
5. come home early from work (or school)
6. miss the bus

7. miss school or work
8. get a haircut
9. take a vacation
10. have a dictation
11. take a test
12. go shopping for food

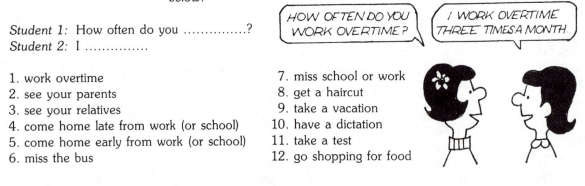

HOW OFTEN DO YOU WORK OVERTIME?

I WORK OVERTIME THREE TIMES A MONTH.

PAIR PRACTICE　*Use adverbial expressions of time with the phrases below.*

Student 1: How many times a .... do you ....?
Student 2: .... a ....

HOW MANY TIMES A MONTH DO YOU GET A PAYCHECK?

TWICE A MONTH.

1. get a paycheck
2. take a shower
3. eat
4. go to a restaurant

5. go to a movie
6. call a friend
7. read a book
8. work

9. clean the house
10. take out the garbage
11. pay your bills
12. ....

---

* Do not use the preposition "in" before these expressions. For example, it is incorrect to say "once in a day."

READ

Here is a page from Carmen's calendar.

FEBRUARY						
S	M	T	W	TH	F	S
1 call parents	2 work, school	3 work, school	4 work, school	5 work, school	6 work, market	7 clean house, date
8 movie date	9 work, school	10 work, school	11 work, school	12 work, school	13 work, paycheck, market	14 clean house
15 call parents	16 holiday, party	17 work, school	18 work, school	19 work, school	20 work, market	21 clean house, restaurant
22 call parents	23 work, school	24 work, school	25 work, school	26 work, school	27 work, paycheck, date	28 clean house, market

PAIR PRACTICE   *Talk with another student. Use the calendar above.*

Student 1: How often does Carmen ....?
Student 2: ....

HOW OFTEN DOES CARMEN HAVE A DATE?

ABOUT THREE TIMES A MONTH.

PAIR PRACTICE   *Use **always**, **usually**, **often**, **sometimes**, and **seldom**. Use the calendar above.*

Student 1: Does Carmen ever ....?
Student 2: Yes, she does. She ....
                  or
    No, she doesn't. She never ....

DOES CARMEN EVER GO TO THE MOVIES?

YES, SHE DOES. SHE USUALLY GOES ABOUT ONCE A MONTH.

PAIR PRACTICE   *Talk about your own monthly schedules.*

Student 1: How often do you ....?
Student 2: I ....

HOW OFTEN DO YOU GO TO A RESTAURANT?

I GO ABOUT ONCE A MONTH.

LISTEN

Carmen is taking a break. Vic Pontrelli is coming into the lunch room.

Carmen: Vic, you're all wet. How is it outside?
Vic: It's terrible. It's raining and windy.
Carmen: Does it rain very often here?
Vic: Not very often, but when we have a winter storm, it rains hard.
Carmen: Isn't it always warm and sunny in California?
Vic: No, not always. It's usually nice, but the weather's sometimes bad here, too.
Carmen: How are the seasons here?
Vic: It rains in the winter, and it snows in the mountains. It's cloudy, foggy, and cool in the spring. In the summer, it's hot, dry, and sometimes smoggy. My favorite season is the fall or autumn. It's cool at night and warm and clear in the daytime.
Carmen: How hot is it in the summer?
Vic: Here in Los Angeles, it's about 65 degrees Fahrenheit at night and about 80 degrees in the daytime.
Carmen: How many degrees Centigrade is that?
Vic: I don't know. I don't understand Centigrade. ·

UNDERSTAND   *Circle* **True**, **False**, *or* **We don't know**.

1. It's always sunny and warm in California.   True   False   We don't know.
2. It sometimes snows in California.   True   False   We don't know.
3. "Fall" means "autumn."   True   False   We don't know.
4. Vic understands degrees in Fahrenheit.   True   False   We don't know.

CHALLENGE   *What's 65 degrees Fahrenheit in degrees Centigrade?* _____ °C.

---

* To change Fahrenheit to Centigrade (Celsius), subtract 32 and multiply by 5/9.
   To change Centigrade to Fahrenheit, multiply by 9/5 and add 32.
   Examples: $(65°F - 32) \times 5/9 = 18.3°C$
   $(27°C \times 9/5) + 32 = 80.6°F$

READ

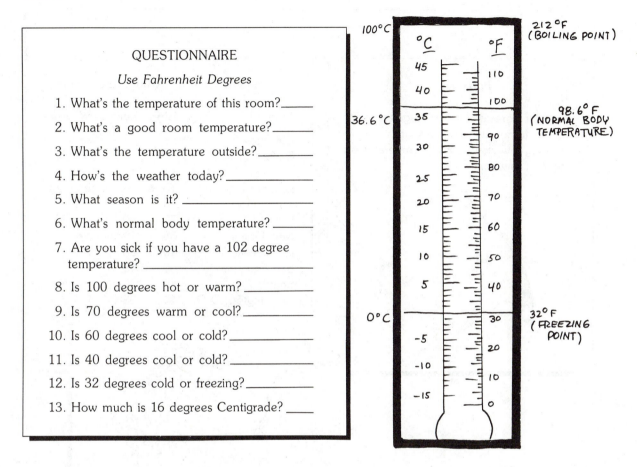

QUESTIONNAIRE

Use Fahrenheit Degrees

1. What's the temperature of this room?_____
2. What's a good room temperature?_____
3. What's the temperature outside?_____
4. How's the weather today?_____
5. What season is it? _____
6. What's normal body temperature?_____
7. Are you sick if you have a 102 degree temperature? _____
8. Is 100 degrees hot or warm?_____
9. Is 70 degrees warm or cool?_____
10. Is 60 degrees cool or cold?_____
11. Is 40 degrees cool or cold?_____
12. Is 32 degrees cold or freezing?_____
13. How much is 16 degrees Centigrade? _____

PAIR PRACTICE   *Talk with another student. Use the thermometer above.*

Student 1: How much is .... degrees Centigrade?
Student 2: It's about .... degrees Fahrenheit.

READ

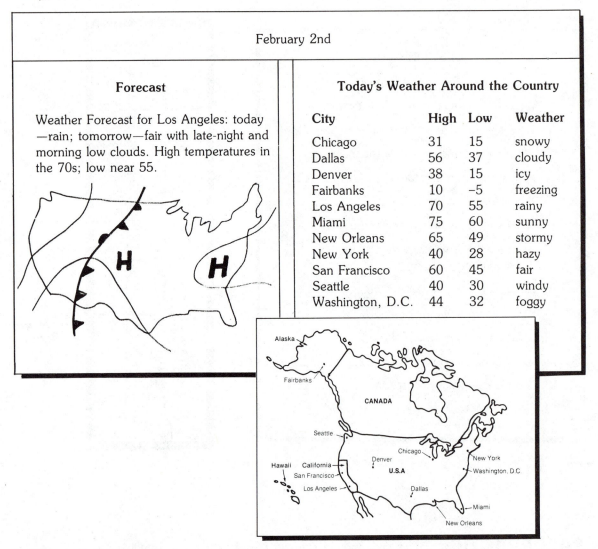

February 2nd

Forecast

Weather Forecast for Los Angeles: today —rain; tomorrow—fair with late-night and morning low clouds. High temperatures in the 70s; low near 55.

Today's Weather Around the Country

City	High	Low	Weather
Chicago	31	15	snowy
Dallas	56	37	cloudy
Denver	38	15	icy
Fairbanks	10	–5	freezing
Los Angeles	70	55	rainy
Miami	75	60	sunny
New Orleans	65	49	stormy
New York	40	28	hazy
San Francisco	60	45	fair
Seattle	40	30	windy
Washington, D.C.	44	32	foggy

PAIR PRACTICE   *Talk with another student. Use the weather forecast and the map above.*

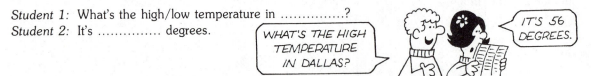

Student 1: What's the high/low temperature in ....?
Student 2: It's .... degrees.

WHAT'S THE HIGH TEMPERATURE IN DALLAS?

IT'S 56 DEGREES.

PAIR PRACTICE   *Use the weather forecast and the map above.*

Student 1: How's the weather in ....?
Student 2: It's ....

HOW'S THE WEATHER IN DALLAS?

IT'S CLOUDY.

CHALLENGE   *Find a weather forecast for your city in the newspaper. Show it to your classmates.*

LISTEN

Carmen begins her training with Betty Kogan.

Betty: I'm glad to meet you, Carmen. Let me show you the shop and your job. It's nice to work here. It isn't dangerous, and the job isn't hard to do. We try to fix circuit boards. When a circuit board doesn't pass inspection, it comes to us. It's expensive to throw away parts, and it's possible to fix some of them. It's interesting to work with electronics, and it's challenging to find the problems, too. Some parts are easy to fix and some are hard to fix. We're able to fix about 80 percent of the boards. After we fix a board, it's necessary to test it. Then it's important to test it a second and a third time before we send it to the shipping department.

UNDERSTAND   *Circle True, False, or We don't know.*

1. Betty likes her job.	True	False	We don't know.
2. Betty is training Carmen.	True	False	We don't know.
3. It's easy to work with electronic parts.	True	False	We don't know.
4. It's dangerous to work with circuit boards.	True	False	We don't know.
5. They are able to fix all the boards.	True	False	We don't know.

GRAMMAR *to be* + Adjective + Infinitive

- *We use the infinitive to complete the meaning of the adjective.*

EXAMPLES	to be	Adjective	Infinitive	
I	'm	glad	to meet	you.
The job	isn't	hard	to do.	
Some parts	are	easy	to fix.	

- *Many sentences with infinitives begin with **it**.*

EXAMPLES

It	's	nice	to work	here.
It	's	expensive	to throw away	the parts.
It	's	challenging	to find	the problems.
It	's	important	to test	it a second time.

READ *Make logical complete sentences with the words in the box.*

It	is / isn't	possible / interesting / hard / easy / important	to begin / to fix / to work / to test / to learn	the broken parts. / a new job. / with you. / English. / early.

WORD BUILDING Negative Prefixes

- *We can change the meaning of a word from affirmative to negative with prefixes (**un-**, **im-**, and **in-**):*

EXAMPLES	Affirmative		Negative		
	1. important	→	unimportant	=	not important
	2. happy	→	unhappy	=	not happy
	3. employed	→	unemployed	=	not employed
	4. expensive	→	inexpensive	=	not expensive
	5. possible	→	impossible	=	not possible

READ *Make logical complete sentences with the words in the box.*

I / He / She / It / You	'm / 's / 're	an	unimportant / uninteresting / impossible / unemployed / inexpensive	book. / problem. / person. / car. / worker.

READ

PAIR PRACTICE

Talk with another student. Use the adjectives under the question with the phrases below.

Student 1: Is it .... to ....?

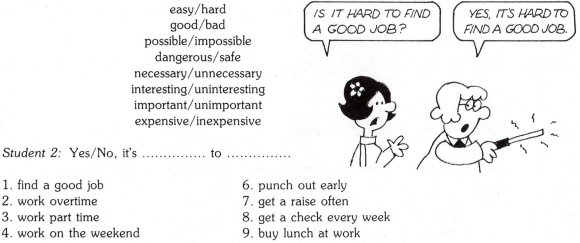

easy/hard
good/bad
possible/impossible
dangerous/safe
necessary/unnecessary
interesting/uninteresting
important/unimportant
expensive/inexpensive

Student 2: Yes/No, it's .... to ....

1. find a good job
2. work overtime
3. work part time
4. work on the weekend
5. come to work on time

6. punch out early
7. get a raise often
8. get a check every week
9. buy lunch at work
10. ....

DISCUSSION

What do you think? Discuss the topics below. Use the adjectives above or others of your own. Answer in your own words.

Student 1: Is it .... to ....?
Student 2: Yes, it is. / No, it isn't.
Student 1: Why?
Student 2: Because ....

1. work well
2. understand people on T.V.
3. begin a new life in a new country
4. find an inexpensive apartment
5. learn to drive a car
6. buy a car

7. pay your bills on time
8. be a millionaire
9. walk outside at night
10. meet some Americans
11. know English well
12. ....

READ

GRAMMAR   too/enough

- *Too* means *excessive*, or *unacceptable*. Use it *before* adjectives.

EXAMPLES   The box is   **too   heavy.**   (I can't lift it.)
I'm   **too   old.**   (I can't pick it up.)

- *Enough* means *sufficient*, or *satisfying*. Use it *after* adjectives.

EXAMPLES   I'm not   **strong   enough.**
Vic's   **strong   enough.**   (He can do the work.)

- *An infinitive often follows an adjective with* **too** *or* **enough** *to show purpose.*

EXAMPLES

I'm   **too weak**   to move the box.
I'm not   **strong enough**   to pick it up.

Note: Do not use *too* or *enough* instead of *very*. *Too* and *enough* imply the idea of a following infinitive.

EXAMPLES   He's   **very strong.**
He isn't   **strong enough**   to pick up the box.
He's   **too weak**   to pick up the box.

READ   Make logical complete sentences with the words in the box.

He She	's	too young young enough	to do the work.
		too old old enough	to work here.
	isn't	too weak strong enough	to pick up the box.

PAIR PRACTICE   *Talk with another student. Use the words below.*

Student 1: Why can't .... work for the company?
Student 2: Because ....

1. weak/strong
2. old/young
3. young/old
4. sick/healthy
5. fat/thin
6. dirty/clean
7. lazy/hard-working
8. messy/neat
9. dangerous/safe
10. dumb/smart
11. small/big
12. big/small

WRITE   *Fill in the spaces below with the words in the box.*

too expensive	twice a month	hours a day	usually
always	once a year	twice a day	never

Carmen is talking to Maria on the telephone.

HOW'S YOUR NEW JOB? TELL ME ABOUT IT.

It's great to work there. I like the job very much. I (1) *always* punch in on time; I'm (2) _____ late. We work eight (3) _____, and we take breaks (4) _____. I (5) _____ bring my lunch with me because it's (6) _____ to buy lunch at a restaurant or snack bar. We get a paycheck (7) _____ and a raise (8) _____.

WRITE   *Put the sentences of the dialog in the correct order. Write the numbers 1 to 9 in front of the sentences (1 is the first in order, and 9 the last).*

_____ What level are you in?

_____ How many times a week does his class meet?

_____ No, I don't, but my husband does.

_____ Level Three.

_____ Oh, really? What does he study?

_____ I study English.

_____ He's studying Spanish.

___1___ Do you go to adult school?

_____ Twice a week. What do you study, Carmen?

DICTATION   *Cover the sentences under each line. Write the dictation on the line as your teacher reads it to you. Then uncover the sentences and correct your writing.*

Dear Mario,

1. _____

   Please pick me up at work today.

2. _____

   I don't want to walk home.

3. _____

   The weather isn't very nice today.

4. _____

   The weather forecast is for rain and wind this afternoon.

5. _____

   See you at 5:00 p.m. in front of the factory.

   Love, Maria

PAIR PRACTICE

Fold the page down the middle. Look only at your side. Do the exercise orally.

Student 1

Listen to the questions from your partner and find the answers in the chart below.

AVERAGE DAILY TEMPERATURES IN JULY AROUND THE COUNTRY

City	High	Low
Chicago	87°F	65°F
Dallas	105	79
Denver	90	63
Los Angeles	80	65
Miami	90	76
New Orleans	95	77
New York	88	71
San Francisco	72	54
Seattle	73	54
Washington, D.C.	91	74

Now ask your partner these questions.

1. How much is 15 degrees Centigrade in Fahrenheit?

2. How much is 100 degrees Fahrenheit in Centigrade?

3. Is 72 degrees Fahrenheit a good room temperature?

4. Is 100 degrees Fahrenheit a comfortable outside temperature?

5. How's the weather today?

6. How much is .... degrees Fahrenheit in Centigrade?

7. How much is .... degrees Centigrade in Fahrenheit?

Student 2

Ask your partner these questions.

1. What's the high temperature in Chicago in July?

2. What's the low temperature in Miami.

3. Is it hot or warm in Dallas?

4. Where is it nice in July?

5. What's the temperature in New Orleans?

6. Where is it between 65 and 80?

7. Where is it cold?

Now listen to the questions from your partner and find the answers in the chart below.

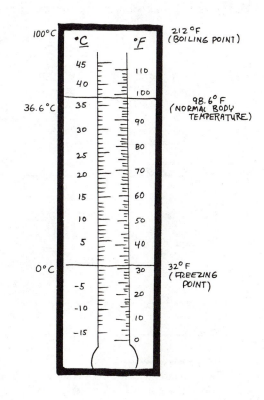

FOLD HERE

WORD BUILDING   Making Adjectives with -y

- *We can sometimes make an adjective from a noun by adding a **-y** at the end of the word.*

  EXAMPLES   sun   ⟶   sunny* weather
                  rain   ⟶   a   rainy   day
                  ice   ⟶   an   icy**   street

WRITE   *Change these nouns to adjectives.*

1. snow   *snowy*

2. ice   _____

3. haze   _____

4. fog   _____

5. smog   _____

6. wind   _____

7. storm   _____

8. cloud   _____

9. rain   _____

WRITE   *What kind of days do the pictures show?*

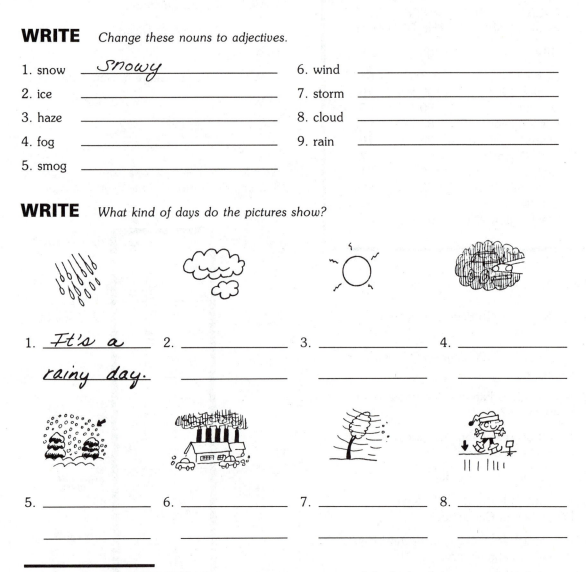

1. *It's a rainy day.*

2. _____

3. _____

4. _____

5. _____

6. _____

7. _____

8. _____

---

*   When a word ends in a consonant-vowel-consonant pattern and the final vowel is stressed, the last consonant is doubled before adding "-y."

** When a word ends in a silent "e," drop the "e" before adding "-y."

WHAT DO I HAVE TO DO TO GO TO COLLEGE?

COMPETENCIES	• Identifying Career Goals and School Subjects
	• Reading an Appointment Book
GRAMMAR	• *have to/has to*
	• *if* clause
	• *in order to*
	• *so*
	• *without*
VOCABULARY	• Common Professions
	• School Subjects
WORD BUILDING	• Suffixes Used in Occupations

LISTEN

Tan Tran and his son, Phuong, are talking at home.

    Tan: Phuong, before you leave the house, you have to take out the garbage.
Phuong: Do I have to?
    Tan: Yes, you do.
Phuong: Dad, I have to have ten dollars.
    Tan: For what?
Phuong: To go out with Ann Wong.
    Tan: Go out!? Why do you have to go out? Why aren't you studying?
Phuong: Why do I always have to study?
    Tan: Do you want money?
Phuong: Yes, of course.
    Tan: Good. If you want money, you have to get a part-time job. If you want a
job, you have to look for a job. If you look for a job, you have to go on an
interview. If you go on an interview, you have to have skills and know
English well. If you want to have skills and know English well, you have to
go to school. If you go to school, you have to study. Right?
Phuong: I guess so.
    Tan: Don't you want to go to college?
Phuong: Yes, of course.
    Tan: Then, you have to study really hard!

UNDERSTAND   *Circle **True**, **False**, or **We don't know**.*

1. Phuong has a job.	True	False	We don't know.
2. Phuong's studying now.	True	False	We don't know.
3. Phuong likes to study.	True	False	We don't know.
4. Phuong has work skills.	True	False	We don't know.
5. "I guess so" means "I think you're right."	True	False	We don't know.

WRITE   *Underline the words **have to** and **has to** each place they appear in the dialog above.*

GRAMMAR *have to/has to*

- *We use **have to** to show necessity or strong obligation.*

- *The third person affirmative singular is irregular: **has to**.*

- ***Have to/has to** are followed by the simple form of the verb.*

EXAMPLES	have to/has to	Verb	
You	**have to**	**take out**	the garbage.
I	**have to**	**have**	ten dollars.
Why do I	**have to**	**study**	all the time?
He	**has to**	**get**	a job.
You	**have to**	**look**	for a job.
Phuong	**has to**	**go**	on an interview.
You	**have to**	**have**	some skills.
Phuong	**has to**	**know**	English well.
You	**have to**	**go**	to school.
You	**have to**	**study.**	

READ *Make logical complete sentences with the words in the box.*

I		study		I		a job.
You	have to	find a job		you		money.
He		go on an interview	if	he	want	to be happy.
She		have work skills		she		to get a job.
We	has to	look for a job		we	wants	to work here.
They		know English		they		to live here.

READ *Make questions with the words in the box. Then answer them.*

		I		study?
	do	he		work?
		she		have work skills?
Why		we	have to	know English?
	does	you		get a job?
		he		go on an interview?
		they		

PAIR PRACTICE   *Talk with another student. Use the phrases below.*

Student 1: Before you leave, you have to ....
Student 2: Do I have to?
Student 1: Yes, you do.

1. take out the garbage
2. clean your room
3. clear the dinner table
4. wash the dishes
5. close the windows

6. help me
7. put on a sweater
8. turn off the radio
9. tell me where you're going
10. ....

> BEFORE YOU LEAVE, YOU HAVE TO TAKE OUT THE GARBAGE.
> YES, YOU DO.
> DO I HAVE TO?

PAIR PRACTICE   *Use the phrases below. Answer in your own words.*

Student 1: Why do I have to ....?
Student 2: Because ....

1. take out the garbage
2. study
3. go to college
4. have skills
5. know English well

6. get a part-time job
7. go to school
8. always stay home
9. do housework
10. ....

> WHY DO I HAVE TO TAKE OUT THE GARBAGE?
> BECAUSE IT'S YOUR JOB.

PAIR PRACTICE   *Use the phrases below. Answer in your own words.*

Student 1: Don't you want to ....?
Student 2: Yes, of course.
Student 1: Then, you have to ....

1. go to college
2. have money
3. be an important person
4. find a good job
5. learn

6. be happy
7. help us at home
8. go visit your friends
9. speak well
10. ....

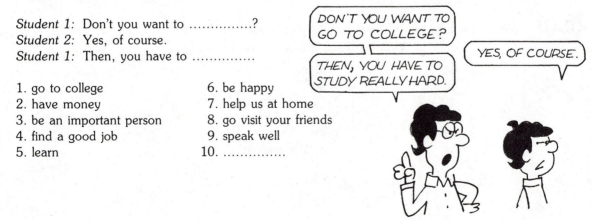

> DON'T YOU WANT TO GO TO COLLEGE?
> THEN, YOU HAVE TO STUDY REALLY HARD.
> YES, OF COURSE.

READ

Phuong and his mother, Lan, are talking.

Lan: What do you want to be?

Phuong: I don't know.

Lan: You have to decide soon, before you go to college. Don't you want to be a doctor?

Phuong: What do you have to study to be a doctor?

Lan: You have to study medicine.

Phuong: I think I want to be an engineer.

Lan: Do you have plans for college?

Phuong: No, I don't.

Lan: Why don't you speak to your counselor at school?

POSSIBLE PROFESSIONS

Career	Subjects
lawyer	law
doctor	medicine
draftsperson	drafting
administrator	management
social worker	psychology, social work
engineer	engineering
computer programmer	computer programming
accountant	accounting, mathematics
scientist	science
artist	art

UNDERSTAND   *Circle True, False, or We don't know.*

1. Phuong wants to be a doctor.   True   False   We don't know.
2. You have to study mathematics if you want to be an accountant.   True   False   We don't know.
3. Phuong's in his last year of high school.   True   False   We don't know.

PAIR PRACTICE   *Talk with another student. Use the list above.*

Student 1: What do I have to study to be a ....?

Student 2: You have to study ....

READ

Phuong is talking to his school counselor.

EXCUSE ME, MA'AM. CAN I MAKE AN APPOINTMENT TO SEE YOU TOMORROW?

I CAN'T STAY NOW. I HAVE TO GO TO MY HISTORY CLASS.

WE CAN TALK NOW. I HAVE A FEW MINUTES.

LET ME CHECK MY APPOINTMENT BOOK. OK. COME IN TOMORROW AFTER SCHOOL.

PAIR PRACTICE   *Talk with another student. Use the phrases below.*

Student 1: Why can't you stay?
Student 2: I have to ....

WHY CAN'T YOU STAY?

I HAVE TO GO TO MY HISTORY CLASS.

1. go to my history class
2. catch the bus
3. meet a friend
4. go home
5. be home early
6. be home for dinner
7. help my father
8. take a test
9. go to work
10. ....

READ

APPOINTMENT BOOK

8 a.m. *register new students*
9 a.m. *return telephone calls*
10 a.m. *speak to accounting class*
11 a.m. *meet with school principal*
12 noon *have lunch with vice-principal*

1 p.m. *Meet Mr. Rios*
2 p.m. *Correct tests*
3 p.m. *meet Phuong Tran*
4 p.m. *write report*
5 p.m. *pick up kids at nursery school*

PAIR PRACTICE   *Use the appointment book.*

Student 1: What does the counselor have to do at .... o'clock?
Student 2: She has to ....

SHE HAS TO MEET PHUONG TRAN.

WHAT DOES THE COUNSELOR HAVE TO DO AT 3 O'CLOCK?

LISTEN

Phoung is meeting with his counselor.

Counselor: Now, how can I help you?
   Phuong: I want to go to college. Can you help me?
Counselor: Why do you want to go to college?
   Phuong: In order to be an engineer.
Counselor: What college do you want to attend?
   Phuong: UCLA.·
Counselor: You can't go to UCLA without good grades. How are your grades?
   Phuong: I have a B average.··
Counselor: Well, you have to do a lot of things.
   Phuong: What do I have to do first?
Counselor: You have to take a special test and send an application.
   Phuong: Is that all?
Counselor: No, it isn't. To go to UCLA, you have to pass the test with a high score.
   Phuong: Oh!

UNDERSTAND   *Circle **True**, **False**, or **We don't know**.*

1. Phuong has good grades.	True	False	We don't know.
2. Phuong wants to study engineering.	True	False	We don't know.
3. Phuong is in college.	True	False	We don't know.
4. Phuong has to take a test to go to UCLA.	True	False	We don't know.
5. Phuong can't go to UCLA with low grades.	True	False	We don't know.

· The University of California, Los Angeles
·· Grades: A = excellent, B = above average, C = average, D = below average, F = failure

GRAMMAR   *in order to*

- *Use **in order to** to show purpose or reason.*
- ***To** is the shortened form of **in order to**.*

EXAMPLES

I want to go to college	**in order to**	be an engineer.
You have to take a test	**to**	go to UCLA.

READ   *Make logical complete sentences with the words in the box.*

Phuong		take a test		go to UCLA.
He	have to	send an application	in order to	be an engineer.
I		go to college		attend college.
We	has to	pass a test	to	pass the class.
Students		study hard		finish college.

PAIR PRACTICE   *Talk with another student. Use the phrases below. Answer in your own words.*

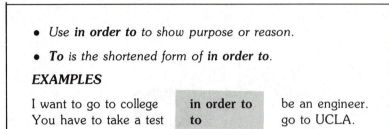

Student 1: Why do you ....?
Student 2: To ....

1. want to go to college
2. have to take tests
3. have to pass the tests
4. come to school
5. want to be an engineer

6. talk to the counselor
7. have to have good grades
8. study hard
9. work
10. ....

WHY DO YOU WANT TO GO TO COLLEGE?

TO BE AN ENGINEER.

PAIR PRACTICE   *Make sentences with **ever**, **never**, and **without**. Supply your own words when necessary.*

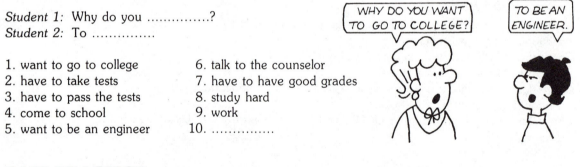

Student 1: Can I ever .... without ....?
Student 2: No, you can never .... without ....

1. go to college/good grades
2. go to work/badge
3. go to school/notebook
4. drive a car/license
5. go shopping/money

6. leave the house/...............
7. eat breakfast/...............
8. go on an interview/...............
9. mail a letter/...............
10. ..../...............

CAN I EVER GO TO COLLEGE WITHOUT GOOD GRADES?

NO, YOU CAN NEVER GO TO COLLEGE WITHOUT GOOD GRADES.

READ

Phuong is playing with his brother.

PAIR PRACTICE

Talk with another student about the things below. Use the verbs in the box to answer the questions.

find	clean	drink	look up	listen	light
mop	know	see	fix	go	call

Student 1: Why do people use ....?
Student 2: To ....

READ

The counselor has an appointment with Mr. Rios.

> I'M MR. RIOS. I HAVE AN APPOINTMENT WITH YOU.
>
> I WANT TO ENROLL MY CHILDREN IN THIS SCHOOL.

> OH, YES. PLEASE COME IN, SIR. WHAT CAN I DO FOR YOU?

The secretary and the counselor are talking after the appointment.

Secretary: How are you?
Counselor: A little tired.
Secretary: Who was that man?
Counselor: That was Mr. Rios. He's new in the city. He has a lot of problems. He has two kids, so he has to enroll them in school. He doesn't have a place to live, so he has to find an apartment fast. He is a widower, so he has to find a person to stay with his kids after school. He doesn't have much money, so he has to find a job. But he has some relatives here, so maybe they can help him.
Secretary: Boy! He sure has a lot of problems.
Counselor: He sure does.

UNDERSTAND   *Circle* **True**, **False**, *or* **We don't know**.

1. Mr. Rios is married.	True	False	We don't know.
2. His wife is dead.	True	False	We don't know.
3. He has relatives in this city.	True	False	We don't know.
4. His relatives can help him.	True	False	We don't know.
5. "He sure does" means "He really does."	True	False	We don't know.

WRITE   *Underline the word* **so** *each place it appears in the dialog above.*

GRAMMAR   *so*

- *We use **so** to show consequence. **Therefore** has a similiar meaning, but it is more formal.*

EXAMPLES

He has two kids,	**so**	he has to enroll them.
He doesn't have a place to live,	**so**	he has to find an apartment.
He doesn't have much money,	**so**	he has to find a job.
He has relatives,	**so**	maybe they can help him.

READ   *Make logical complete sentences with the words in the box.*

Mr. Rios The counselor Phuong	doesn't have money, wants to go to college, is tired, needs help, wants to pass the test,	so	he she	has to	rest. take a test. get a job. study. talk to a counselor.

PAIR PRACTICE   *Talk with another student. Use the phrases below, and answer in your own words.*

Student 1: ....
Student 2: So?
Student 1: So ....

MR. RIOS HAS TWO KIDS.
SO HE HAS TO ENROLL THEM IN SCHOOL.

SO?

1. Mr. Rios has two kids.

2. Mr. Rios has a problem.

3. The kids don't speak English.

4. Phuong's brother wants to be a fireman.

PLEASE, DAD...

5. Phuong need ten dollars.

NO!

6. Phuong's father doesn't want to give him $10.00.

7. Mr. Rios is thirsty.

8. The counselor is tired.

?

9. ....

WRITE   *Fill out the appointment book for today and Sunday. Use the expressions **have to** and **don't have to**.*

APPOINTMENT BOOK
THINGS I HAVE TO DO.

TODAY	SUNDAY
I have to work.	*I don't have to work.*

PAIR PRACTICE   *Talk with another student about the schedule above.*

Student 1: What do you have to do today?
Student 2: I have to ....
Student 1: What about on Sunday?
Student 2: I don't have to ....

WHAT DO YOU HAVE TO DO TODAY?

WHAT ABOUT ON SUNDAY?

I HAVE TO WORK.

I DON'T HAVE TO WORK ON SUNDAY.

PAIR PRACTICE   *Talk about the schedule above.*

Student 1: Do you have to .... today/on Sunday?
Student 2: Yes, I do. / No, I don't.

DO YOU HAVE TO WORK TODAY?

YES, I DO.

WRITE
Put the sentences of the dialog in the correct order. Write the numbers 1 to 10 in front of the sentences (1 is the first in order and 10 the last).

_____ They're very good students.

_____ How are you doing, Mr. Rios?

_____ I have a job and a new apartment.

___*1*___ Hello, this is Mr. Rios.

_____ What about them?

_____ That's wonderful news.

_____ How are they doing?

_____ I'm glad to hear that. I have some good news for you, too.

_____ Fine, thanks, I'm calling to ask about my children.

_____ What good news?

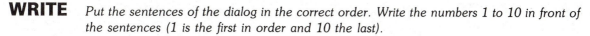

DICTATION
Cover the sentences under each line. Write the dictation on the line as your teacher reads it to you. Then uncover the sentences and correct your writing.

An office memo from the counselor to the secretary.

OFFICE MEMO

TO: Natalie   FROM: Claudine

1. _____

   I'm very busy, so please don't make any appointments for me today.

2. _____

   I have a lot of things to do.

3. _____

   I don't have enough time.

4. _____

   I need the time to write a report.

5. _____

   Please get me Phuong Tran's grades.

6. _____

   I have to have them for his college application.

                              Thanks,
                                   Claudine

PAIR PRACTICE   *Fold the page down the middle. Look only at your side. Follow the instructions.*

Student 1	Student 2

Student 1

Listen to the questions from your partner and find the answers below.

SCHOOL REPORT CARD

NAME: *Phuong Tran*

Subject	Grade
English	B
History	C
Mathematics	A
Physical Education	B
Science	A
Drafting	B

A = excellent   B = above average
C = average   D = below average
F = failure

Your partner fills out your appointment book for you. Tell your partner what you have to do at:

6 a.m.

8 a.m.

10 a.m.

12 noon

2 p.m.

4 p.m.

6 p.m.

8 p.m.

10 p.m.

Student 2

Ask your partner these questions.

1. What's Phuong's grade in English?

2. What's his grade in science?

3. Does he study engineering?

4. Does he have a good grade in history?

5. Does he have a good grade in physical education?

6. What's his grade average?

7. What subjects does he study?

Now fill in the appointment book for your partner. Listen carefully to the information your partner tells you.

THINGS I HAVE TO DO TODAY

6 a.m. _____

8 a.m. _____

10 a.m. _____

12 noon _____

2 p.m. _____

4 p.m. _____

6 p.m. _____

8 p.m. _____

10 p.m. _____

FOLD HERE

WORD BUILDING   Suffixes Used in Occupations

- *We can form many names of occupations by adding the suffix -er to a verb.*

EXAMPLES	*Verb*		*Occupation*
	work	→	work<u>er</u>
	teach	→	teach<u>er</u>
	paint	→	paint<u>er</u>

WRITE   *Fill in the spaces with names of occupations. Use the suffix -er.*

1. A ___*painter*___
   paints buildings.

2. A _____
   writes books.

3. A computer _____
   programs computers.

4. A _____
   builds buildings.

5. A truck _____
   drives trucks.

6. A driving _____
   teaches driving.

7. A _____
   waits on tables.

8. A _____
   reports the news.

9. A _____
   manages people.

WORD BUILDING

- *Other suffixes used in occupations:*

-ist	-or	-ess	-man or -woman
typ<u>ist</u>	doct<u>or</u>	steward<u>ess</u>	police<u>man</u>
art<u>ist</u>	direct<u>or</u>	wait<u>ress</u>	sales<u>man</u>
dent<u>ist</u>	instruct<u>or</u>	act<u>ress</u>	police<u>woman</u>
chem<u>ist</u>	act<u>or</u>		sales<u>woman</u>

CHALLENGE   *How many occupations can you name using the suffixes above?*

_____ _____ _____ _____

_____ _____ _____ _____

_____ _____ _____ _____

CHALLENGE   *Walk around the room and make a list of the occupations of your classmates.*

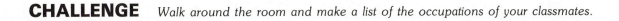

WHAT ARE YOU GOING TO DO TOMORROW?

COMPETENCIES	• Describing Future Events or Activities
GRAMMAR	• Future with the Present Continuous
	• Future with *will*
	• Future with *going to*
	• Prepositions: *in, across, by*
VOCABULARY	• Toys
	• Picnic Food
	• Transport
	• Expressions of Time (Future)
SPELLING	• Double Consonant Combinations

LISTEN

James and Betty Fuller are at home. They're talking about tomorrow's plans.

James: What are you doing tomorrow?

Betty: I'm going shopping to buy a present for Bobby Barns. It's his birthday on Sunday. What about you?

James: I'm playing golf with Roy Barns tomorrow morning. We're planning a school picnic. What are you buying Bobby?

Betty: I'm getting him a toy.

James: Are they having a birthday party?

Betty: Yes, they're giving him a small party on Sunday afternoon.

James: Are you going?

Betty: Yes, we're going.

James: Am I going, too?

Betty: Yes, you're going, too. And we're having dinner at my mother's house afterwards.

UNDERSTAND   *Circle **True**, **False**, or **We don't know**.*

1. Bobby is having a party tomorrow.	True	False	We don't know.
2. Bobby is seven years old.	True	False	We don't know.
3. The Fullers are having dinner with the Barns family tomorrow.	True	False	We don't know.
4. The Fullers are bringing a present.	True	False	We don't know.
5. James is going shopping with his wife.	True	False	We don't know.

WRITE   *Underline all verbs in the present continuous in the sentences above.*

GRAMMAR   Future with the Present Continuous

- *We often use the present continuous to show the near future.*

EXAMPLES

What	**are**	you	**doing**	tomorrow?
I	**'m**		**going**	shopping tomorrow.
I	**'m**		**playing**	golf tomorrow morning.
We	**'re**		**planning**	a class picnic.
What	**are**	you	**buying**	Bobby?
	Are	they	**having**	a party?
They	**'re**		**giving**	him a small party.
	Are	you	**going?**	
We	**'re**		**going.**	
We	**'re**		**having**	dinner at my mother's.

READ   *Make logical complete sentences with the words in the box.*

		bringing	a party	tomorrow.
I	'm	buying	shopping	on Sunday afternoon.
We		having	to dinner	tomorrow morning.
He	's	giving	a picnic	tomorrow afternoon.
She		planning	golf	Sunday evening.
They	're	going	a present	afterwards.
You		playing	at home	later.

PAIR PRACTICE   *Talk with another student. Use the words below. Answer in your own words in the present continuous.*

Student 1: What are you doing ....?
Student 2: I'm ....

1. tomorrow
2. tonight
3. tomorrow morning
4. tomorrow afternoon
5. tomorrow evening
6. the day after tomorrow

7. this weekend
8. next Saturday
9. next Sunday
10. next week
11. next month
12. next ....

LISTEN

Betty Fuller is talking to Nancy Barns on the telephone.

Betty: How's everything?
Nancy: We're busy. I have to do a million things before Bobby's party tomorrow.
After the housework, my daughter and I will go to the market. We'll buy the
food for the party, and then we'll come home and get ready for the party.
Betty: Will you make a birthday cake?
Nancy: No, I won't, but Patty will. And Roy will do all the work tomorrow, too. I
won't have to clean up after the party, I won't wash the dishes, and I won't
make dinner.
Betty: Why not?
Nancy: Because tomorrow is my birthday, too!

UNDERSTAND   *Circle **True**, **False**, or **We don't know**.*

1. Nancy and her son, Bobby, will have a birthday tomorrow.   True   False   We don't know.
2. Nancy and her daughter, Patty, will go shopping before
   they do the housework.   True   False   We don't know.
3. Bobby will go shopping with Nancy.   True   False   We don't know.
4. Roy will make dinner tomorrow.   True   False   We don't know.
5. Nancy will make a birthday cake.   True   False   We don't know.
6. Nancy won't work tomorrow.   True   False   We don't know.

WRITE   *Underline **will**, **won't**, and **'ll** in the sentences above.*

GRAMMAR   Future with *will*

- *We use* **will** *and* **won't** *to show future time, especially of plans and promises.*

- **Won't** *is the contraction of* **will not**, *and* **'ll** *is the contraction of* **will**.

- **Will** *is a modal. We form the affirmative, question, and negative forms of* **will** *in the same way as for* **can** *and* **must**.

EXAMPLES   *Affirmative*

My daughter and I	**will**	**go**	to the supermarket.
We	**'ll**	**buy**	food for the party.
We	**'ll**	**go**	home.
We	**'ll**	**get ready**	for the party.
Roy	**will**	**do**	all the work tomorrow.
Tomorrow	**will**	**be**	my birthday, too.

Question

| **Will** | you | **make** | a birthday cake? |

Short Answers

No, I **won't,** but Theresa **will.**

Negative

I	**won't**	**clean up**	after the party.
I	**won't**	**wash**	the dishes.
I	**won't**	**make**	dinner.

READ   *Make logical complete sentences with the words in the boxes.*

Bobby		be	my birthday	on Sunday.
Roy	will	go	to a party	on the weekend.
I		buy	a party	tomorrow.
Patty	'll	work	all the work	tomorrow afternoon.
Nancy		do	a cake	this afternoon.
Betty	won't	have	shopping	after the housework.
It		make	a present	too.

		do	a party	
	they	buy	shopping	
	you	make	a present	today?
Will	Roy	have	a cake	on Sunday?
	Patty	work	dinner	tonight?
	Betty	go	all the work	tomorrow?
	Nancy	give	a birthday	
	Bobby			

Yes,	I	will.
	he	
	she	
No,	they	won't.
	we	

READ

James and Betty are talking about Nancy's present.

WHAT WILL YOU BUY NANCY FOR HER BIRTHDAY?

MAYBE I'LL BUY HER A BLOUSE.

PAIR PRACTICE   *Talk with another student about the items below.*

Student 1: What will you buy Nancy?
Student 2: Maybe I'll buy her ....

WHAT WILL YOU BUY NANCY?

MAYBE I'LL BUY HER A BLOUSE.

1. a blouse   2. a plant   3. an appointment book   4. a sweater

5. some glasses   6. a record   7. some stationery   8. an address book

READ

HOW MUCH IS THIS BLOUSE?

GOOD, I'LL TAKE IT.

IT'S FIFTEEN DOLLARS.

THAT'LL BE FIFTEEN DOLLARS PLUS TAX.

PAIR PRACTICE   *Use the pictures in the preceding Pair Practice.*

Student 1: How much is this ....?
Student 2: It's $...............
Student 1: Good, I'll take it.
Student 2: That'll be $...............

HOW MUCH IS THIS BLOUSE?

GOOD, I'LL TAKE IT.

IT'S FIFTEEN DOLLARS.

THAT'LL BE FIFTEEN DOLLARS PLUS TAX.

READ

Betty is at a toy store.

HOW OLD IS HE?

I WANT TO BUY A TOY FOR A BOY.

HE'LL BE SEVEN YEARS OLD TOMORROW.

TOYS

PAIR PRACTICE   *Talk with another student. Use the phrases below.*

Student 1: How old is/are ....?
Student 2: He/She/They'll be ....

HOW OLD IS HE?

HE'LL BE SEVEN YEARS OLD TOMORROW.

1. Bobby Barns/7/tomorrow
2. Nancy Barns/35/tomorrow
3. Patty Barns/14/next week
4. José Corral/6/next month

5. Phuong Tran/17/next June
6. Roberto and Raymond Monte/25/next July
7. Sami Hamati/49/next September
8. David Fernandez/23/next November

GROUP DISCUSSION   *What do you think? Is it OK to ask the age of children, young adults, or people over 40? Why or why not?*

READ

HERE'S A NICE BALL.

WILL THAT BE ALL?

GOOD, I'LL TAKE IT.

YES, THAT'LL BE IT.

PAIR PRACTICE   *Talk with another student. Use the words and pictures below.*

Student 1: Here's a ....
Student 2: I'll take it.
Student 1: Will that be all?
Student 2: Yes, that'll be it.

HERE'S A NICE BALL.

WILL THAT BE ALL?

I'LL TAKE IT.

YES, THAT'LL BE IT.

1. ball
2. game
3. coloring book
4. toy car
5. doll
6. doll house
7. train
8. bat

WRITE   *When will your birthday be? What will you do on your birthday? What won't you do? Write your answers below.*

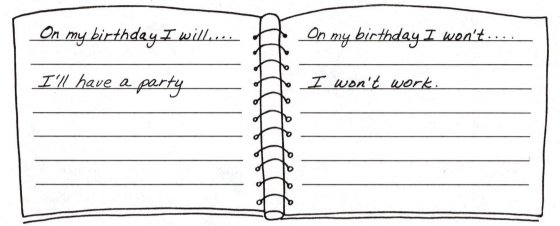

On my birthday I will....

I'll have a party

On my birthday I won't....

I won't work.

READ

At the party.

HAPPY BIRTHDAY TO YOU,
HAPPY BIRTHDAY TO YOU,
HAPPY BIRTHDAY, DEAR
BOBBY AND NANCY,
HAPPY BIRTHDAY TO YOU!

Nancy is telling Betty about the special present she is getting.

Nancy: Thank you very much for the present. It's beautiful.
Betty: You're very welcome.
Nancy: Guess what!
Betty: What?
Nancy: I'm going on a trip!
Betty: Where are you going?
Nancy: Across the country. It's a birthday present from Roy.
I'm leaving next month.

UNDERSTAND   *Circle **True**, **False**, or **We don't know**.*

1. Betty will go on a trip with Roy.	True	False	We don't know.
2. Betty will leave next week.	True	False	We don't know.
3. Nancy likes Betty's present.	True	False	We don't know.

READ

Here is Nancy's itinerary.

March 1-3
- fly to Las Vegas
- play cards at a casino

March 4-5
- fly to Denver
- walk in the mountains

March 6-7
- fly to Chicago
- visit museums
- go to a jazz club

March 8-9
- take a bus to New York
- go to a Broadway show
- buy a suit or dress

March 10-11
- take a bus to Boston
- go sightseeing

March 12-15
- take a train home
- travel 4 days by train
- relax on the train
- look at the view
- read a book

March 16
- arrive in Los Angeles
- take a taxi home

PAIR PRACTICE   *Talk with another student. Ask and answer questions about Nancy's itinerary.*

Where will you go on March 1?
How will you get to Las Vegas?
What will you do in Las Vegas?
Where will you go on ....?
How will you get ....?
What will you do in ....?

I'll go to Las Vegas.
I'll fly.
I'll play cards at a casino.
I'll go to ....
I'll ....
I'll ....

GRAMMAR   Prepositions *by* and *across*

- *We use **by** to show means of transportation. Nancy will go to Boston **by bus**.*

- ***Across** means from one side to the other side. Boston is **across the country** from Los Angeles.*

PAIR PRACTICE

*Talk with another student, using the words and pictures below. Use **by** in the answers.*

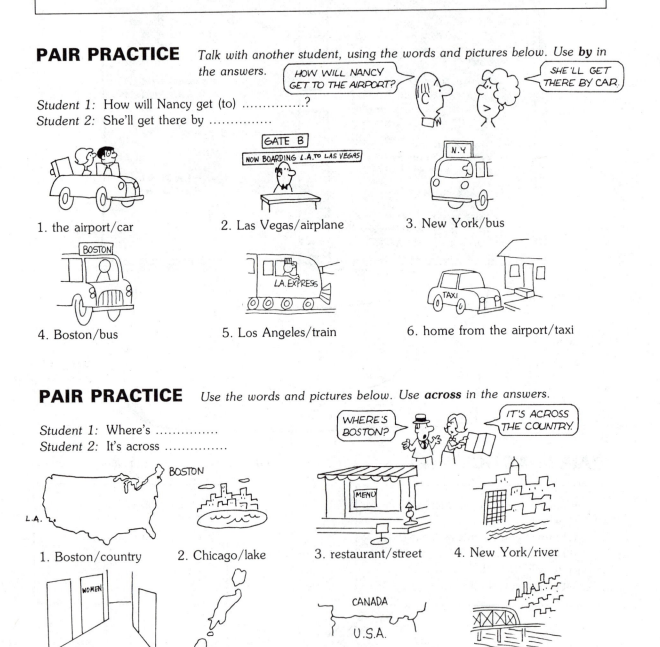

Student 1: How will Nancy get (to) ....?
Student 2: She'll get there by ....

1. the airport/car

2. Las Vegas/airplane

3. New York/bus

4. Boston/bus

5. Los Angeles/train

6. home from the airport/taxi

PAIR PRACTICE

*Use the words and pictures below. Use **across** in the answers.*

Student 1: Where's ....
Student 2: It's across ....

1. Boston/country

2. Chicago/lake

3. restaurant/street

4. New York/river

5. the restrooms/hall

6. Japan/ocean

7. Canada/border

8. San Francisco/bridge

LISTEN

Roy Barns and James Fuller are playing golf.

   Roy: What are we going to do for our class picnic?

James: When is it going to be?

   Roy: It's going to be in two weeks.

James: Where are we going to have it?

   Roy: The students want to go to the lake.

James: OK. What are we going to need?

   Roy: My students are going to bring the meat and drinks. And what about your students?

James: They're going to bring salads and desserts.

   Roy: Who's going to bring the paper goods?

James: I'm going to bring the plates, cups, and tableclothes.

   Roy: And I'm going to bring plastic utensils and napkins, OK?

James: Good. I think we're going to have a good time.

UNDERSTAND *Circle **True**, **False**, or **We don't know**.*

1. The picnic is going to be next week.	True	False	We don't know.
2. The picnic is going to be at the lake.	True	False	We don't know.
3. The students are going to bring the food.	True	False	We don't know.
4. James is going to bring the drinks.	True	False	We don't know.
5. The married students are going to bring their kids.	True	False	We don't know.
6. Roy is going to bring spoons, forks, knives, and napkins.	True	False	We don't know.

GRAMMAR   Future with *going to*

- • *We use **going to** to show a future action.*

- • *We use the verb **to be** before **going to** and a simple verb after it.*

- • ***Going to** is sometimes pronounced "gonna" in informal speech.*

EXAMPLES	to be		going to	Simple Verb	
What	**are**	we	**going to**	**do**	about the picnic?
When	**is**	it	**going to**	**be?**	
It	**'s**		**going to**	**be**	in two weeks.
What	**are**	we	**going to**	**need?**	
My students	**are**		**going to**	**bring**	meat and drinks.
They	**'re**		**going to**	**bring**	salads and desserts.
Who	**'s**		**going to**	**bring**	the paper goods?
I	**'m**		**going to**	**bring**	plastic utensils.
We	**'re**		**going to**	**have**	fun.

- • *We often use the preposition **in** to show a future time.*

EXAMPLE   *The party is going to be*   **in**   *two weeks.*

READ   *Make logical complete sentences with the words in the box.*

I	'm		be	there.
The students			bring	at the lake.
They	's	going to	go	to the lake.
The picnic			have	food.
We	're		buy	fun.
It	are		eat	in two weeks.

PAIR PRACTICE   *Talk with another student using the phrases below. Use the preposition **in** in the answers.*

Student 1: When's .... going to be?
Student 2: It's going to be in ....

WHEN'S THE PICNIC GOING TO BE?

IT'S GOING TO BE IN TWO WEEKS.

1. the picnic/two weeks
2. the party/three weeks
3. the trip/one month
4. the test/a few days
5. the dictation/a few minutes
6. dinner/a few hours
7. the birthday/a few days
8. the T.V. program/one hour
9. lunch/fifteen minutes
10. the movie/half an hour
11. the vacation/one year
12. ..../..............

READ

Here's a list of the people going to the picnic and what they are bringing.

NAME	FOOD
PICNIC	
Mr. Barn's class	
Roy and Nancy Barns (+2 kids)	utensils
Wanda and Stephen Bratko (+2 kids)	hamburgers
Sami Hamati	juice
Maria and Mario Corral (+2 kids)	hot dogs
Li and Yen Chu	chicken
TAN AND LAN TRAN	beef
Miko Takahashi	iced tea
Rita Landry	soda
Mr. Fuller's class	
David Fernandez	green salad
Joanne Yates (+ friend)	potato salad
Paul Green	cake
Ray Monte (+wife)	cookies
Roberto Monte	potato chips

PAIR PRACTICE   *Talk with another student. Use the list above.*

Student 1: What is/are .... going to bring?
Student 2: He/She/They .... going to bring ....

WHAT'S SAMI GOING TO BRING?

HE'S GOING TO BRING SOME JUICE.

PAIR PRACTICE   *Use the list above.*

Student 1: Is/Are .... going to bring ....?
Student 2: Yes/No, ...

ARE MARIA AND MARIO GOING TO BRING CHICKEN?

NO, THEY AREN'T, THEY'RE GOING TO BRING HOT DOGS.

WRITE   *Write sentences with* **going to** *on the lines below.*

Roy and James are talking.

Roy: Maria and Mario are sitting at the picnic table. They're really hungry.
James: What are they going to do?
  Roy: *They're going to eat.*

James: Miko's plate is empty.
  Roy: What's she going to do?

James: _____

  Roy: Theresa's at the lake. She's wearing a bathing suit.
James: What's she going to do?

  Roy: _____

James: Sami's thirsty.
  Roy: What's he going to do?

James: _____

  Roy: Paul Green's full.
James: What's he going to do?

  Roy: _____

James: We're finished.
  Roy: What are we going to do?

James: _____

  Roy: I'm tired. What about you?
James: So am I. What are we going to do?

  Roy: _____

WRITE *Fill in the spaces with* **will**, **won't**, *or* **want**.

Tan: Do you _want_ to take a walk?

Lan: Not right now. I _will_ take a walk later.
I _want_ to rest now.

Wanda: Do you _____ some potato salad?

Stephen: Sure, and I _____ some chicken, too.
I'm really hungry, so I _____ come
back for more food later.

Maria: What do you _____ to do?

Theresa: I _____ to go swimming.

Maria: Don't swim too far!

Theresa: OK, I _____.

James: _____ we go to your mother's for
dinner again next Sunday?

Betty: Why? Don't you _____ to go?

James: No, I don't. I _____ to take you
out to dinner.

Sami: _____ you be in class tomorrow?

Miko: Yes, I _____. Why?

Sami: I have to work overtime, so I can't
come to school.

Miko: Do you _____ me to call you and
tell you the homework?

Sami: Thanks. I _____ be home at 10 p.m.
Call me then.

WRITE   *What are your plans for next week? What are you going to do? Write your plans below.*

THINGS I'M GOING TO DO NEXT WEEK

Monday: _____

_____

Tuesday: _____

_____

Wednesday: _____

_____

Thursday: _____

_____

Friday: _____

_____

Saturday: _____

_____

Sunday: _____

_____

PAIR PRACTICE   *Talk with another student about the schedule above. Answer the second question in your own words.*

Student 1: What are you going to do on ....?
Student 2: I'm going to ....
Student 1: Why are you going to do that?
Student 2: Because ....

WRITE   *Put the sentences in the dialog in the correct order. Write the numbers 1 to 7 in front of the sentences (1 is the first in order and 7 the last).*

The Barns family is in the car. They're going home.

_____ Who do you want to invite?

_____ When is it going to be?

___*1*___ Are we going to have a picnic again?

_____ A friend from school.

_____ Yes, we're going to have a picnic again very soon.

_____ Sure, I like the beach. Will you let me invite a friend?

_____ In June at the beach. Is that OK?

DICTATION   *Cover the sentences under each line. Write the dictation on the line as your teacher reads it to you. Then uncover the sentences and correct your writing.*

Nancy is writing a postcard to a friend in New York.

Nancy Barns
18 513 Park Street
Los Angeles, Ca. 91403
Dear Joan,

1. _____

   I'm going to be in your city next month.

2. _____

   Please send me some information.

3. _____

   Where can I stay? How's the weather?

4. _____

   What kind of clothes will I need to bring?

5. _____

   What is there to see in your city?

6. _____

   Send me the information at the address above.

   your friend,
   Nancy

WRITE   *Address the envelope. Use your own address. Answer Nancy's questions. Write about your city.*

FROM: _____

_____

_____

_____

TO: _____

_____

_____

_____

salutation

_____ } your address

_____

_____ ← today's date

Dear _____

_____

_____

_____ } body

_____

_____

_____

_____

_____ ← closing

_____

PAIR PRACTICE   *Fold the page down the middle. Look only at your side.*

Student 1

Listen to the questions from your partner and find the answers below.

> **BETTY AND JAMES FULLER'S WEEKEND TRIP TO MEXICO**
>
> **Friday:**
> - drive to Ensenada, Mexico
> - stay at Amigo Hotel
> - eat at Casa Rosa restaurant
>
> **Saturday:**
> - go fishing in morning
> - go shopping in the afternoon
> - go to night club in evening
>
> **Sunday:**
> - drive back to Los Angeles
> - get ready for Monday

Your partner will fill out your schedule book for tomorrow. Tell your partner what you're going to do at:

1. 6:00 o'clock in the morning
2. 8:00 o'clock in the morning
3. 10:00 o'clock in the morning
4. 12:00 noon
5. 2:00 o'clock in the afternoon
6. 4:00 o'clock in the afternoon
7. 6:00 o'clock in the afternoon
8. 8:00 o'clock in the evening
9. 10:00 o'clock in the evening

Student 2

Ask your partner these questions.

1. How are James and Betty Fuller going to get to Ensenada?
2. What are they going to do on Friday?
3. Where will they stay?
4. Where are they going to eat?
5. How many days are they going to stay?
6. How are they getting back to Los Angeles?
7. When are they going to go back?

Write out your partner's schedule below as he/she tells it to you.

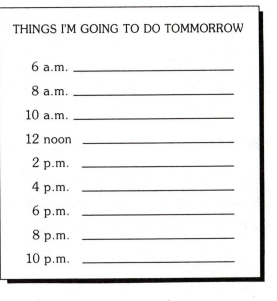

THINGS I'M GOING TO DO TOMMORROW

6 a.m. _____

8 a.m. _____

10 a.m. _____

12 noon _____

2 p.m. _____

4 p.m. _____

6 p.m. _____

8 p.m. _____

10 p.m. _____

SPELLING   Double Consonant Combinations

- *The **l** and **s** sounds are usually spelled with double letters after one vowel letter.*

EXAMPLES

fall   bell   bill   full

glass   mess   miss   boss

- *The following words are exceptions to this rule. Remember them.*

is   gas   yes   this   us   bus   plus

WRITE   *Fill in the spaces with double **ss** or **ll**.*

1. I wi*ll*__ ca____ the bo____ and te____ him to fi____ a____ the ta____ wine gla____es.

2. Do____s and ba____s se____ we____ in the fa____.

3. Please clean off the me____ on the wa____ acro____ from the be____ in the ha____.

5

WHERE WERE YOU ABOUT ELEVEN O'CLOCK?

COMPETENCIES	• Reporting a Robbery • Describing Emotions • Describing Levels of Difficulty
GRAMMAR	• Past Tense of *to be* (was/were)
VOCABULARY	• Office Equipment • Time Expressions (Past Tense) • Emotions • Descriptive Adjectives
PRONUNCIATION	• The *w* and *v* Sounds

LISTEN

It's Monday evening at the adult school. Mona Boulos is speaking to Rita Landry about yesterday's picnic.

Mona: Were you at the picnic yesterday?
Rita: Yes, I was.
Mona: How was it?
Rita: It was wonderful.
Mona: Where was it?
Rita: It was at the lake.
Mona: How was the weather?
Rita: It was fantastic. It was warm and sunny.
Mona: How long were you there?
Rita: We were there all day.
Mona: Who was there?
Rita: Everybody was there.
Mona: Were Maria and Wanda there?
Rita: Yes, they were, and their families were there, too. Why weren't you there?
Mona: I wasn't at the picnic because I was sick in bed with a cold.
Rita: That's too bad. Maybe next time.

UNDERSTAND   *Circle **True, False,** or **We don't know.***

1. Mona was at the picnic.	True	False	We don't know.
2. Mona's friends were at the picnic.	True	False	We don't know.
3. Mona was at home yesterday.	True	False	We don't know.
4. The weather at the picnic was good.	True	False	We don't know.
5. Everybody was sick yesterday.	True	False	We don't know.
6. Mona's husband was at home yesterday.	True	False	We don't know.

WRITE   *Underline **was, were, wasn't,** and **weren't** in the sentences above.*

GRAMMAR   Past Tense of *to be*

- *We use* **was** *with* **I, he, she,** *and* **it**.

- *We use* **were** *with* **you, we,** *and* **they**.

EXAMPLES

	Affirmative				*Question*	
I	**was**	at the picnic.			**Were**	you at the picnic?
The picnic	**was**	wonderful.	How		**was**	it?
It	**was**	at the lake.	Where		**was**	the picnic?
It	**was**	fantastic.	How		**was**	the weather?
We	**were**	there all day.	Who		**was**	there?
They	**were**	there, too.	Why		**were**	Wanda and Maria there?

	Negative			*Short Answers*	
I	**wasn't**	there because I was sick.	Yes, I	**was.**	
Why	**weren't**	you there?	Yes, they	**were.**	
			No, I	**wasn't.**	
			No, they	**weren't.**	

READ   *Make logical complete sentences with the words in the boxes.*

The picnic		sick	
I	was	at the picnic	yesterday.
Everybody	wasn't	there	yesterday morning.
Maria and Wanda	were	wonderful	yesterday afternoon.
We	weren't	in bed with a cold	yesterday evening.
They		at the lake	all day.
Mona			
It			

Was	you	at the picnic		
	Mona	at home		
	Maria and Wanda	sick in bed		
	Sami	at the lake	yesterday?	
	the picnic	good		
Were	the weather	with their families		

Yes,	I	was.	
	he	wasn't.	
	she	were.	
	it	weren't.	
No,	we		
	they		

PAIR PRACTICE   *Talk with another student. Use the words and pictures below.*

Student 1: How was the ....?
Student 2: It was ....

1. picnic/wonderful   2. lake/cold   3. food/delicious   4. temperature/warm

5. area/clean   6. weather/fantastic   7. park/big   8. day/great

PAIR PRACTICE   *Use the words and pictures below.*

Student 1: How was/were ....?
Student 2: He/She/They ....

1. Mr. Barns and
   Mr. Fuller/busy

2. Paul Green/full   3. Miko/happy   4. Sami/sleepy

5. Wanda and Stephen/
   tired

6. Theresa/afraid   7. Maria/worried   8. kids/quiet

READ

PAIR PRACTICE   *Ask about the foods below. Find the answers in the picture above.*

Student 1: Was/Were there ....?
Student 2: Yes/No, there ....

1. potato salad
2. bananas
3. hamburgers
4. soup
5. cake
6. milk

7. hot dogs
8. potato chips
9. beer
10. cookies
11. juice
12. ice cream

WRITE   *Fill in the spaces with questions. The answers will help you figure out the questions.*

Yen Chu and Mona are talking about the picnic.

Mona: Hi, Yen. <u>*Were you at the picnic*</u>?

Yen: Yes, I was at the picnic.

Mona: _____?

Yen: The weather was very nice.

Mona: _____?

Yen: All the students were there.

Mona: _____?

Yen: Yes, David was there.

Mona: _____?

Yen: No, Carmen wasn't there. _____?

Mona: I was sick all last week with a cold.

Yen: I'm sorry to hear that.

LISTEN

It's Tuesday evening. Sami is asking Rita Landry about yesterday's class.

Rita: Where were you yesterday?

Sami: I was at work, and I have to work overtime again tomorrow. How was the class yesterday?

Rita: It was OK. There was a surprise quiz.

Sami: There was? How was it?

Rita: It wasn't very easy. It was complicated and a little confusing.

UNDERSTAND   *Circle **True**, **False**, or **We don't know**.*

1. Sami wasn't in class on Monday.	True	False	We don't know.
2. Sami has to work overtime again tonight.	True	False	We don't know.
3. A quiz is a short test.	True	False	We don't know.
4. The quiz was difficult.	True	False	We don't know.

PAIR PRACTICE   *Talk with another student. Use the words and pictures below.*

Student 1: How was the quiz?

Student 2: It was ....

1. complicated   2. confusing   3. easy   4. hard

5. simple   6. difficult   7. long   8. fair

WRITE   *Match the questions with their answers.*

1. Were the directions simple?
2. Was the quiz easy?
3. Was it long?
4. Were the grades high?
5. Was it unfair?

a. No, it was short.
b. No, it was fair.
c. No, they were low.
d. No, it was difficult.
e. No, they were complicated.

WRITE   *Answer the questions in the questionnaire with the adjectives in the box.*

easy	hard	long	short	clear	confusing
fair	simple	complicated	unfair	difficult	

QUESTIONNAIRE

1. How was your last test? _____

2. How was your homework? _____

3. How was your last quiz? _____

4. How is the registration process at your school? _____

5. How are the directions in this book? _____

6. How are the exercises in this book? _____

7. Are the chapters too long? _____

8. Was your last dictation easy? _____

9. Are the lessons too complicated? _____

10. How's your class? _____

11. Are your tests fair or unfair? Why? _____

_____

LISTEN

The school principal is calling the police about a robbery at school.

Principal: Hello, Police Department? My name's Lanny Nelms. I'm the principal of the adult school. I want to report a robbery.

Officer: Where was the robbery?

Principal: It was here in the adult school office.

Officer: When was it?

Principal: Last night.

Officer: Was there a security guard on duty?

Principal: No, there wasn't.

Officer: What can you tell me about the robbery?

Principal: All the office equipment was here last night, and now it isn't.

Officer: I'll send a police officer right there.

UNDERSTAND   *Circle True, False, or We don't know.*

1. It's Wednesday.   True   False   We don't know.
2. The robbery was on Tuesday night.   True   False   We don't know.
3. The officer is at the school.   True   False   We don't know.
4. The office equipment was there yesterday.   True   False   We don't know.

WRITE   *Fill in the spaces with was, were, wasn't, or weren't.*

The students are talking about the robbery.

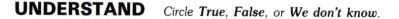

Rita: There ___*was*___ a robbery last night.

Miko: Oh, really? _____ it at your home?

Rita: No, it _____. It _____ here, and the office equipment is missing.

Wanda: What time _____ the robbery?

Rita: I don't know. I think it _____ very late.

Maria: _____ the security guards here?

Rita: No, they _____ here last night. They usually go home at ten o'clock.

READ

The police officer is writing her report.

Officer: Do you have a picture of the office before the robbery?
Principal: Yes, I do. Here's one.

Here's the main office now.

PAIR PRACTICE   *Talk with another student. Use the two pictures above.*

Student 1: What's the problem?
Student 2: There was/were .... in the office
before the robbery, but now there isn't/aren't.

PAIR PRACTICE

Give the location of the office equipment below before the robbery. Use the picture on the previous page.

Student 1: Now tell me. Where was/were the ....?
Student 2: It was/They were ....

1. typewriters
2. file cabinet
3. clocks
4. computer
5. computer printer
6. adding machine
7. cash register
8. calculators
9. pencil sharpener
10. staplers
11. safe
12. telephone answering machine
13. desk lamps
14. ....

WRITE

Write sentences in the correct order from the words below each line.

There's a witness!

Witness: *I have some information about the robbery.*
the robbery/have/about/I/some information/.

Officer: _____
have/do/you/What kind/information/of/?

Witness: _____
a strange man/behind/the school/was/There/last night/.

Officer: _____
time/he/What/there/was/?

Witness: _____
was/about/He/eleven/there/p.m./at

Officer: _____
you/know/this/do/How/?

Witness: _____
see/I/can/from my bedroom window/the school/.

Officer: _____
you/Will/that man/recognize/if you see him again/?

Witness: _____
know/I'll/Sure/him/,/.

Officer: _____
for/Thanks/help/your/.

READ

The witness is looking at some pictures at the police station.

WRITE   *Fill in the spaces with **was**, **were**, **wasn't**, or **weren't**.*

Later that day...

Officer: OK, Max, where _____were_____ you about eleven o'clock last night?

Max: I _____ with a sick friend.

Officer: _____ you and your sick friend at home all night?

Max: Yes, we _____. Why?

Officer: _____ you and your sick friend near the adult school last night?

Max: No, we _____. We _____ at home.

Officer: A witness says you _____ behind the adult school about 11 p.m.

Max: No! I _____ there, I tell you. I _____ at home!

Officer: Why is there office equipment in your apartment?

Max: OK! OK! OK! It _____ me.

PAIR PRACTICE   *Fold the page down the middle. Look only at your side. Do the exercise orally.*

Student 1	Student 2

Student 1

Listen to the questions from your partner and find the answers in the picture below.

Now ask your partner these questions about the principal's schedule yesterday.

1. Where was the principal at 1 p.m.?

2. Where was the principal at 5 p.m.?

3. Where was he at 3 p.m.?

4. Who was with the principal at dinner time?

5. Was he in his office at 6 p.m.?

6. When was he in Mr. Fuller's class?

7. Where was he at 9 p.m.?

8. Was he in his office at 2 pm.?

Student 2

Ask your partner these questions.

1. Where's the typewriter?

2. Is the computer in front of or next to the printer?

3. Is the pencil sharpener above or below the file cabinet?

4. Is the telephone answering machine on or under a table?

5. Is the adding machine behind or between the typewriters?

6. Where's the file cabinet?

Listen to the questions from your partner and find the answers in the principal's appointment book below.

APPOINTMENT BOOK

DATE: *Monday*

1 p.m. { *meeting with secretaries*
2 p.m. { *in my office*
3 p.m. { *write reports in*
4 p.m. { *my office*
5 p.m. { *dinner with counselor*
6 p.m. { *at the snack bar*
7 p.m. *visit Mr. Barn's class*
8 p.m. *visit Mr. Fuller's class*
9 p.m. { *meeting with teachers*
10 p.m. { *in teachers' room*

FOLD HERE

PRONUNCIATION   The *w* and *v* Sounds

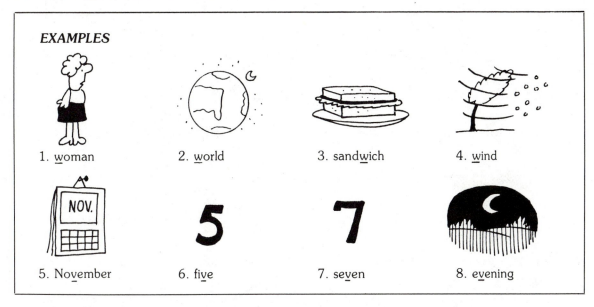

EXAMPLES

1. <u>w</u>oman   2. <u>w</u>orld   3. sand<u>w</u>ich   4. <u>w</u>ind

5. No<u>v</u>ember   6. fi<u>v</u>e   7. se<u>v</u>en   8. e<u>v</u>ening

WRITE   *Fill in the spaces with* **w** *or* **v**.

1. Why <u>W</u>ere you <u>w</u>ith that <u>w</u>oman for fi<u>v</u>e <u>w</u>eeks on your <u>v</u>acation?

2. How ____ill the ____eather be on No____ember ele____enth and t____elfth?

3. He ____orks ____ery ____ell ____ithout ____isits from la____yers.

4. Those se____en ____omen ____ill ____isit his ____ife e____ery ____ednesday.

5. ____e ____ant you to open the ____est ____indow in the e____ening.

THANK YOU, BUT NO THANK YOU

COMPETENCIES	• Describing Past Actions
	• Reading a Time Card
	• Reading a Personal Schedule
GRAMMAR	• Regular Verbs in the Past Tense
VOCABULARY	• Common Work Vocabulary
	• Expressions of Time *(ago, last)*
PRONUNCIATION	• The *-ed* Ending
SPELLING	• Rules for Adding the *-ed* Ending

LISTEN

Sami Hamati is an auto mechanic. He is telling David Fernandez about his job.

David: Did you attend class last night?

Sami: No, I didn't. My boss asked me to work overtime in our new paint department at the garage. I stayed and earned a few extra dollars. I wanted to come to school, but I decided the work was important. I learned a new skill.

David: What kind of skill?

Sami: How to paint cars.

David: Oh, really?

Sami: Yes, I tried to paint my car last week, but I didn't do a very good job.

David: What happened?

Sami: I didn't use the right kind of paint, and I didn't mix it enough. When I picked up the can of paint, I dropped it and it spilled all over my car. I wiped off some paint, but it didn't help. My car looked terrible. All the guys at the garage laughed, and we joked about it all week.

David: What did you do?

Sami: I waited until the next day. The bad paint dried, and the guys showed me how to paint a car correctly. I repainted my car, and now it looks great. I improved a lot. Do you want me to paint your car?

David: Thank you, but no thank you!

UNDERSTAND   *Circle True, False, or We don't know.*

1. David attended class last night.	True	False	We don't know.
2. Sami worked a few extra hours overtime.	True	False	We don't know.
3. Sami is learning how to paint cars.	True	False	We don't know.
4. Sami's car is new.	True	False	We don't know.
5. David wants Sami to paint his car.	True	False	We don't know.

GRAMMAR   Regular Verbs in the Past Tense

- *We add the **-ed** ending to form the past tense of regular verbs in the affirmative only. Do not use the **-ed** ending with verbs in the question and negative forms.*

EXAMPLES   *Affirmative*

My boss	**asked**	me to work overtime.
I	**wanted**	to come to school.
I	**decided**	the work was important.
I	**painted**	my car.
I	**picked**	up the can of paint.
I	**dropped**	it.
It	**spilled**	all over my car.
I	**tried**	to wipe off the paint.
The guys	**laughed.**	
We	**joked**	about it.
I	**waited**	until the next day.
The paint	**dried.**	
The guys	**showed**	me how to paint correctly.
I	**improved**	a lot.

- *We use **did** to signal the question.*

- *We use **did not** to signal negatives. **Didn't** is the contraction of **did not**.*

	Negative				*Question*	
I	**didn't do**	a good job.			**Did**	you attend class?
I	**didn't use**	the right paint.	What		**did**	you do?
I	**didn't mix**	it enough.				

Short Answers   *Did you attend class?*   **Yes, I did.**   *or*   **No, I didn't.**

READ   *Make logical sentences with the words in the boxes.*

The car	used	the wrong paint.
Sami	joked	the right paint.
The guys	painted	about my mistake.
The boss	didn't use	his car.
David	didn't joke	David's car.
I	didn't paint	paint.

	you	work	overtime?
	Sami	drop	the paint?
Did	David	paint	over the car?
	the boss	spill	a new skill?
	the guys	learn	about the problem?

Yes,	I	did.
	he	
	it	
No,	they	didn't.

PRONUNCIATION   The *-ed* Ending

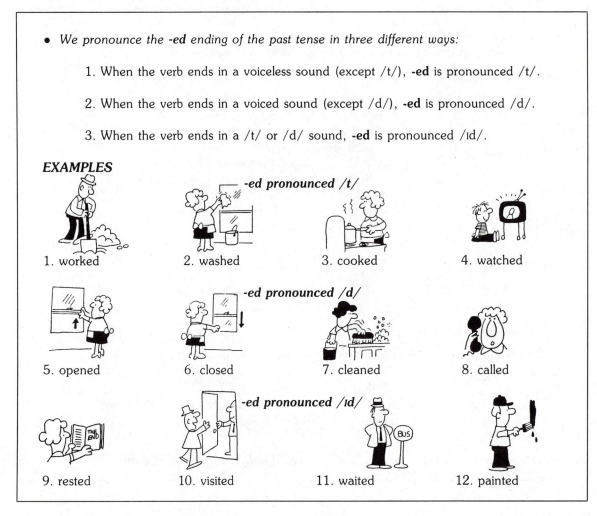

- *We pronounce the **-ed** ending of the past tense in three different ways:*

  1. When the verb ends in a voiceless sound (except /t/), **-ed** is pronounced /t/.

  2. When the verb ends in a voiced sound (except /d/), **-ed** is pronounced /d/.

  3. When the verb ends in a /t/ or /d/ sound, **-ed** is pronounced /ɪd/.

EXAMPLES

-ed pronounced /t/

1. worked   2. washed   3. cooked   4. watched

-ed pronounced /d/

5. opened   6. closed   7. cleaned   8. called

-ed pronounced /ɪd/

9. rested   10. visited   11. waited   12. painted

READ   *Pronounce the words in the list below. Be careful with the endings.*

1. stayed	9. decided	17. listened	25. started	33. spilled
2. played	10. dressed	18. lived	26. thanked	34. painted
3. asked	11. ended	19. looked	27. visited	35. joked
4. called	12. finished	20. loved	28. moved	36. watched
5. cleaned	13. helped	21. needed	29. waited	37. washed
6. closed	14. learned	22. practiced	30. wanted	38. cooked
7. opened	15. showed	23. rained	31. washed	39. arrived
8. danced	16. liked	24. rested	32. poured	40. returned

CHALLENGE   *How many complete sentences can you make with the verbs in the list above?*

READ

1. He opened the can of paint.

2. He mixed the paint.

3. He picked up the can.

4. He poured the paint.

5. He dropped the can.

6. The paint spilled.

7. He wiped off the paint.

8. He cleaned the floor.

9. He waited until the next day.

10. The paint dried.

11. He repainted the car.

12. The car looked great.

PAIR PRACTICE   *Talk with another student about Sami's activities above.*

Student 1: What happened first?
Student 2: ....
Student 1: Then what happened?
Student 2: ....
Student 1: Then what happened?
Student 2: ....

PAIR PRACTICE   *Ask questions using the pictures above. Answer with short answers.*

Student 1: Did ....?
Student 2: Yes/No, ...

PAIR PRACTICE   *Talk with another student. Use the phrases below.*

Student 1: What did the guys show you how to do?
Student 2: They showed me how to ....

1. paint cars
2. mix paint
3. open a can
4. do a good job
5. work well
6. joke about problems

7. use paint
8. repaint a car
9. speak English
10. laugh
11. help people
12. ....

PAIR PRACTICE   *Use the phrases below.*

Student 1: Did you ever learn how to .... when you lived at home?
Student 2: Yes, I did. / No, I didn't.

1. swim
2. drive a car
3. paint
4. cook
5. wash clothes
6. use a computer

7. use simple tools
8. clean the house
9. fix things
10. make a cake
11. make clothes
12. ....

PAIR PRACTICE   *Ask about the items below. Use the words in the box to answer.*

Student 1: How does the .... look?
Student 2: It looks ....!

terrible	fantastic	good	OK
dirty	wonderful	bad	nice
damaged	old	new	great

WRITE   *Match the questions with their answers.*

1. What did you mix?
2. How long did you work?
3. What did you learn?
4. What did you drop?
5. Whose car did you paint?
6. Who laughed?
7. What kind of paint did you use?
8. Who asked you to work overtime?

a. A new skill.
b. A few hours.
c. The guys.
d. The paint.
e. The wrong kind.
f. The boss.
g. The can.
h. Mine.

READ

TIME CARD

NAME: *Sami Hamati*   DATES: From *2/16* To *2/23*

	Sun.	Mon.	Tue.	Wed.	Thur.	Fri.	Sat.	WEEK
Regular Hours:	0	8	8	8	8	8	0	40
Overtime:	0	1	1.5	2	2	1.5	3	11
Total:	0	9	9.5	10	10	9.5	3	51

PAIR PRACTICE   *Talk with another student. Use the time card above.*

Student 1: How many hours did Sami work on ....?
Student 2: He worked ....

HOW MANY HOURS DID SAMI WORK ON WEDNESDAY?

HE WORKED EIGHT HOURS PLUS TWO HOURS OVERTIME.

PAIR PRACTICE   *Use the time card above.*

Student 1: Did Sami work overtime on ....?
Student 2: Yes, he did. / No, he didn't.

DID SAMI WORK OVERTIME ON SUNDAY?

NO, HE DIDN'T.

LISTEN

Miko and Sami are talking before class.

Sami: Hi, Miko, what are you doing?
Miko: I'm writing a letter to my cousin, Yoshi, in Japan.
Sami: Didn't she study here last semester?
Miko: No, she didn't. Yoshi visited the United States last year. She was here
    because she wanted to improve her English. She's a translator and she needs
    English in her work. She arrived in June, and she stayed three months. We
    both studied English in a summer program at UCLA. We really enjoyed our
    classes. We lived in a dormitory on campus. We traveled around the state on
    the weekends. She returned home in September, and I stayed here. I miss
    her very much.
Sami: Will she come back?
Miko: I don't know. Maybe she will. She wants to come back next summer.

UNDERSTAND   *Circle **Yes, she did.** or **No, she didn't**.*

1. Miko studied English last summer.	Yes, she did.	No, she didn't.
2. Miko lived in Japan.	Yes, she did.	No, she didn't.
3. Yoshi stayed here.	Yes, she did.	No, she didn't.
4. Miko traveled around California.	Yes, she did.	No, she didn't.
5. Miko returned to Japan with Yoshi.	Yes, she did.	No, she didn't.
6. Miko lived at UCLA.	Yes, she did.	No, she didn't.

WRITE   *Underline all verbs in the **past tense** in the sentences above.*

WRITE   *Circle all the verbs in the **present tense** in the sentences above.*

WRITE   *Put a box around all the verbs in the **future tense** in the sentences above.*

WRITE   *Help Sami ask Miko questions. The answers will help you figure out the questions.*

Sami: *When did Yoshi arrive* _____?
Miko: Yoshi arrived in June.

Sami: _____?
Miko: Because she wanted to improve her English.

Sami: _____?
Miko: We studied English.

Sami: _____?
Miko: We studied at UCLA.

Sami: _____?
Miko: Our class started at nine o'clock in the morning.

Sami: _____?
Miko: It ended at three o'clock in the afternoon.

Sami: _____?
Miko: We traveled around the state.

Sami: _____?
Miko: Yoshi returned to Japan last September.

Sami: _____?
Miko: I stayed here because I want to improve my English.

READ

Sami and Miko are talking about last month.

Miko: I didn't answer Yoshi's letter last month, so I have to answer it now.
Sami: Why were you busy? What did you do?
Miko: I worked overtime. I cleaned my apartment. I visited some senior citizens at a nursing home. I played tennis. I washed my car. I moved to a new apartment, and I painted my living room.
Sami: I see. You were really busy.

UNDERSTAND   *Circle **True** or **False**.*

1. Senior citizens are people over 65 years old.	True	False
2. All senior citizens live in nursing homes.	True	False
3. Miko learned how to drive a car.	True	False
4. Miko knows how to play tennis.	True	False
5. Miko knows how to paint.	True	False

WRITE   *Help Miko answer the questions. Use short answers.*

1. Sami: Did you paint the furniture?   Miko: *No, I didn't.*

2. Sami: Did you clean your apartment?   Miko: *Yes, I did.*

3. Sami: Did you play football?   Miko: _____

4. Sami: Did you work?   Miko: _____

5. Sami: Did you visit some friends?   Miko: _____

6. Sami: Did you fix your car?   Miko: _____

7. Sami: Did you move?   Miko: _____

8. Sami: Did you answer Yoshi's letter?   Miko: _____

READ

Here is Miko's calendar for last month.

FEBRUARY						
Sunday	Monday	Tuesday	Wednesday	Thursday	Friday	Saturday
1 walk in the park	2 work overtime	3 attend exercise class	4 answer some letters	5 clean apartment	6 cook dinner for friends	7 move to new apartment
8 Call parents	9 watch special T.V. program	10 Visit library	11 start to read new book	12 finish work early	13 visit senior citizens	14 play tennis
15 visit museum	16 No work	17 finish book	18 invite friends to dinner	19 rain, stay home	20 paint living room	21 shop for new dress
22 relax at home	23 work late	24 attend exercise class	25 work overtime	26 shop for food	27 visit senior citizens	28 play tennis

PAIR PRACTICE   *Talk with another student. Use the calendar.*

Student 1: What did Miko do on ....?
Student 2: She ....

PAIR PRACTICE   *Use the calendar.*

Student 1: Did she ....?
Student 2: Yes, she did. / No, she didn't.

PAIR PRACTICE

*Talk with another student. Use the phrases below. Notice how **ago** is used in the answers.*

Student 1: When did you last ....?
Student 2: I .... ago. What about you?
Student 1: I ....
            or
        I never ....

1. visit a museum
2. start to read a new book
3. answer a letter
4. wash windows
5. call your relatives

6. work late
7. move to this city
8. clean your apartment
9. invite people to your home
10. ....

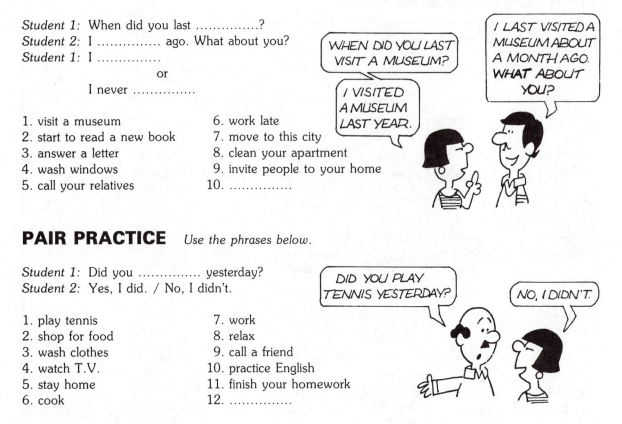

WHEN DID YOU LAST VISIT A MUSEUM?

I VISITED A MUSEUM LAST YEAR.

I LAST VISITED A MUSEUM ABOUT A MONTH AGO. **WHAT ABOUT YOU?**

PAIR PRACTICE

Use the phrases below.

Student 1: Did you .... yesterday?
Student 2: Yes, I did. / No, I didn't.

1. play tennis
2. shop for food
3. wash clothes
4. watch T.V.
5. stay home
6. cook

7. work
8. relax
9. call a friend
10. practice English
11. finish your homework
12. ....

DID YOU PLAY TENNIS YESTERDAY?

NO, I DIDN'T.

PAIR PRACTICE

Ask and answer original questions with the words in the box.

ask	close	dance	decide	end	finish
help	learn	listen	live	open	play
rest	start	study	use	walk	talk
laugh	joke	enjoy	travel	return	arrive

I ARRIVED HERE A FEW MONTHS AGO.

Student 1: When did you ....?
            or
        Where did you ....?
            or
        What did you ....?
            or
        Why did you ....?
            or
        How did you ....?
Student 2: I ....

WHEN DID YOU ARRIVE HERE?

WRITE   *Fill in the spaces with* ***-ed***, ***-d***, ***did***, *or* ***didn't***. *Leave some spaces empty.*

Miko is asking Sami about his past.

Miko: What about you, Sami? I don't know very much about you. When *did*

you immigrate *X* to this country?

Sami: I immigrate *d* here a few months ago.

Miko: Where *did* you live *X* before?

Sami: I live *d* in Egypt.

Miko: _____ you live____ alone?

Sami: No, I _____. I live____ with my relatives.

Miko: _____ you live____ in Cairo?

Sami: Yes, I _____.

Miko: _____ you work____ in Cairo, too?

Sami: No, I _____. I work____ in a garage outside of the city.

Miko: _____ you work____ every day?

Sami: I work____ six days a week; I _____ work____ on Friday.

Miko: _____ you like____ your job?

Sami: Yes, I _____.

Miko: _____ you like____ your house and relatives?

Sami: Of course, I _____.

Miko: Why _____ you move____ here?

Sami: I move____ here because I want____ to start a new life.

SPELLING   Rules for Adding the *-ed* Ending

- *If the word ends in a silent* **e**, *only add* **-d**.

EXAMPLES   live → liv<u>ed</u>   joke → jok<u>ed</u>   like → lik<u>ed</u>

- *If the word ends in a consonant +* **y** *pattern, change the* **y** *to* **i** *and add* **-ed**. *If the* **y** *follows a vowel, simply add* **-ed**.

EXAMPLES   **y** *changes to* **i**   **y** *after a vowel*

study → stud<u>ied</u>   play → play<u>ed</u>
marry → marr<u>ied</u>   stay → stay<u>ed</u>
dry → dr<u>ied</u>   enjoy → enjoy<u>ed</u>

- *When a word ends in a consonant-vowel-consonant pattern and the final vowel is stressed, the last consonant is doubled before adding* **-ed**. *A final* **w**, **x**, *or* **y** *is never doubled.*

EXAMPLES   **Consonant Doubled**   **Not Doubled**

shop → shop<u>ped</u>   fix → fix<u>ed</u>
drop → drop<u>ped</u>   need → need<u>ed</u>
stop → stop<u>ped</u>   pick → pick<u>ed</u>

WRITE   *Fill in the spaces with the past tense of the verbs under the lines. Don't forget to make all necessary spelling changes.*

I'm Sami Hamati. When I was in Egypt, I ___*lived*___ and ___*worked*___ in Cairo.
          live   work

I _____ Egypt, but I _____ to come to this country to start a new
     like   decide

life. I _____ here a few months ago, but my relatives _____ in
     move   stay

Egypt. When I _____ in Los Angeles, I _____ for a job, and I was
          arrive   apply

lucky because I _____ to work immediately. I _____ at the adult
          start   register

school because I _____ to study English. I _____ to learn English
          want   try

quickly because I _____ it for my work. I _____ every day, _____
          need   practice   study

very much, and _____ many questions. Today my English isn't too bad.
          ask

WRITE   *Answer the questionnaire.*

QUESTIONNAIRE

1. What school did you attend last semester? _____

2. When did your last class end? _____

3. Did your English improve in your last class? _____

4. What book or books did you use in your last class? _____

_____

5. When did you register for this class? _____

6. When did you start your present class? _____

7. Why did you decide to come to this school? _____

_____

8. How did you learn about this school? _____

_____

9. Did you study English before you arrived in this country? _____

10. What kind of school did you attend in your country? _____

11. What subjects did you study in your country? _____

12. Where did you live before you moved here? _____

13. Where did you work before you moved here? _____

14. Why did you move to this country? _____

_____

7

IT'S NICE TO BE BACK HOME

COMPETENCIES	• Describing Past Actions
	• Identifying Major Cities and States
GRAMMAR	• Irregular Verbs in the Past Tense
VOCABULARY	• Common Irregular Verbs
	• The Preposition *through*
	• U.S. Cities, States, and Areas
WORD BUILDING	• The Prefix *re-*

LISTEN

Nancy Barns and Betty Fuller are having lunch. Nancy is telling Betty about her trip.

Betty: How was your trip?

Nancy: It was wonderful.

Betty: Where did you go, and what did you do?

Nancy: I went around the country, but I had an especially good time my last night in New York City.

Betty: What did you do there?

Nancy: My sister and her husband live there, you know. Well, they took me to dinner at a famous restaurant. We ate a delicious meal, and we drank champagne. We had a great time. Then, my sister gave me a present.

Betty: What did she give you?

Nancy: She bought tickets for a Broadway show. We finished dinner a little late, and we didn't want to be late for the show, so we took a taxi to the theater. We were very lucky because just as we got there, the show began.

Betty: What kind of show did you see?

Nancy: We saw a musical, and we sat in the front row, too.

Betty: What musical was it?

Nancy: I forgot the name, but it was a wonderful show.

Betty: What did you do afterward?

Nancy: Nothing much. We went back to my sister's house. The next morning my brother-in-law drove me to the train station and I left New York.

UNDERSTAND   *Circle True, False, or We don't know.*

1. Nancy had a good time in New York.	True	False	We don't know.
2. Nancy went to dinner after the show.	True	False	We don't know.
3. She walked to the theater.	True	False	We don't know.
4. Nancy's sister lives near the theater.	True	False	We don't know.
5. Nancy took a train from New York.	True	False	We don't know.
6. Nancy knows the name of the musical.	True	False	We don't know.

GRAMMAR Irregular Verbs in the Past Tense

- *We use the base form of the verb (infinitive without **to**) in the question and negative forms.*

Base Form

Question:	Did you	**go**	to San Francisco?
Negative:	No, I didn't	**go**	to San Francisco.

- *We use **did** to signal the question and **didn't** to signal the negative.*
- *We use the irregular forms only in the affirmative form.*

Irregular Form

Affirmative: I   **went**   to New York.

Base Form		Irregular Form
go	→	went
have	→	had
take	→	took
eat	→	ate
drink	→	drank
buy	→	bought
get	→	got
forget	→	forgot
see	→	saw
sit	→	sat
begin	→	began
drive	→	drove
leave	→	left
give	→	gave

READ *Make logical complete sentences with the words in the boxes.*

Did	Nancy Nancy's sister she you they the show	eat drink begin sit leave get forget	the name of the show? in the front row? champagne? a delicious dinner? when they got there? to the theater on time? New York the next morning?

Yes, No,	she it they I we	did. didn't.

I Nancy Nancy's sister Her brother-in-law She They	went had saw bought took drove	some theater tickets. Nancy to the train station. to a famous restaurant. a Broadway show. a taxi to the theater. a present for Nancy.

READ

1. Her sister bought theater tickets.

2. They went to a famous restaurant.

3. They ate a meal and drank champagne.

4. Nancy's sister gave her a present.

5. They took a taxi to the theater.

6. They got to the theater.

7. They sat in the front row.

8. The show began.

9. They saw a musical.

10. Nancy had a good time.

11. Her brother-in-law drove her to the station.

12. Nancy left New York.

PAIR PRACTICE   *Talk with another student. Use the pictures above.*

Student 1: What did .... do?
Student 2: He/She/They ....

WHAT DID NANCY'S SISTER DO?

SHE BOUGHT SOME THEATER TICKETS.

PAIR PRACTICE   *Use the pictures above.*

Student 1: What/Where/When did ....?
Student 2: He/She/They ....

WHAT DID NANCY SEE?

SHE SAW A MUSICAL.

PAIR PRACTICE   *Use the pictures above.*

Student 1: Did ....?
Student 2: Yes, ... did.
              or
          No, ... didn't.

DID NANCY BUY THE THEATER TICKETS?

NO, SHE DIDN'T

PAIR PRACTICE   *Talk with another student. Use the phrases below.*

Student 1: Did you .... ?
Student 2: Yes, I did. / No, I didn't.

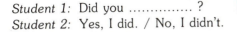

DID YOU GO TO A FAMOUS RESTAURANT?

YES, I DID.

1. go to a famous restaurant
2. take a friend to dinner
3. eat a delicious meal
4. drink champagne
5. get a nice present

6. go to a Broadway musical
7. sit in the front row of the theater
8. go to New York
9. take a train
10. forget the show's name

PAIR PRACTICE   *Use the phrases below. Add your own words when necessary. Use **ago** or **last** in the answers.*

Student 1: When did you ....?
Student 2: I .... ago/last ....

WHEN DID YOU EAT IN A RESTAURANT?

I ATE IN A RESTAURANT TWO WEEKS AGO.

1. eat in a restaurant
2. drive or take a bus to school
3. have a good time
4. get to a movie or show late
5. begin this course
6. leave your country

7. see ....
8. give ....
9. go to ....
10. forget ....
11. eat ....
12. buy ....

WRITE   *Fill in the spaces with the correct form of the verbs in the past tense.*

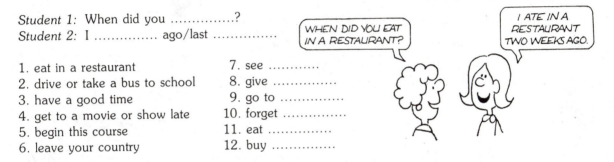

1. *Did* you eat well in New York?
2. _____ you take taxis in New York?
3. _____ you go to museums?
4. _____ you give your sister a present?
5. _____ you see any movies?
6. _____ you drive a car in New York?
7. _____ you leave early in the morning?
8. _____ you buy any presents?

Yes, I *ate* very well.

Yes, I _____ taxis.

Yes, I _____ to a few.

Yes, I _____ her a sweater.

No, I _____ _____ any movies.

No, I _____ _____ there.

Yes, I _____ at 7 a.m.

Yes, I _____ a present for you!

WRITE   *Fill in the spaces below with the words in the box.*

Betty is asking more questions about Nancy's trip.

did	didn't	go	went
eat	ate	drink	drank

Betty: When _did_ you _go_ to the restaurant?

Nancy: We _went_ at six o'clock in the evening.

Betty: How _____ you _____ to the restaurant?

Nancy: We _____ in my brother-in-law's new car.

Betty: What time _____ you _____ to the theater?

Nancy: We _____ to the theater at eight p.m., but we _____

_____ by car. We took a taxi.

Betty: What kind of food _____ you _____ at the restaurant?

Nancy: I _____ fish, and my sister and her husband _____ chicken.

Betty: _____ you _____ any dessert?

Nancy: No, I _____ _____ any dessert, but my brother-in-law

_____ some cake.

Nancy: We _____ some very good champagne.

Betty: _____ you _____ French champagne?

Nancy: No, we _____ _____ French champagne. We _____

some very good champagne from California.

Betty: How much champagne did you _____ ?

Nancy: We _____ only one bottle.

WRITE   *Fill in the spaces below with the words in the box.*

did	didn't	give	gave
see	saw	have	had

Betty: _____ your sister _____ you a present before or after dinner?

Nancy: She _____ it to me after dinner.

Betty: What _____ you _____ her?

Nancy: I _____ her a beautiful sweater.

Betty: _____ you _____ your brother-in-law a sweater, too?

Nancy: No, I _____ _____ him a sweater; I _____ him

a shirt from California.

Betty: What _____ you _____ in New York?

Nancy: I _____ the Statue of Liberty.

Betty: _____ you _____ the World Trade Center?

Nancy: No, I _____ _____ that, but I _____

the Empire State Building.

Betty: What else _____ you _____?

Nancy: I _____ Rockefeller Center.

Betty: _____ you really _____ a good time?

Nancy: Yes, I _____ a wonderful time.

Betty: _____ you _____ time to see your other relatives?

Nancy: No, I _____ _____ enough time to see all of them.

They live outside the city.

LISTEN

Nancy is telling Betty about her trip back on the train.

HOW WAS YOUR TRIP?

Betty: How was your trip back?
Nancy: It was a very restful three-day trip. I did very little. I slept late in the morning, relaxed, read a good book, and wrote some letters.
Betty: What else did you do?
Nancy: Sometimes I sat in the sightseeing car and looked at the scenery.
Betty: What did you see from the train?
Nancy: I saw a lot of interesting places: cities, mountains, and deserts.
Betty: Did you speak to any people?
Nancy: Sure. I met and spoke to a lot of nice passengers on the train. I had dinner with some people. And I made some friends, too.
Betty: Are you glad to be back?
Nancy: All in all, I like to travel, but it's nice to be home.

UNDERSTAND   *Circle **True**, **False**, or **We don't know**.*

1. Nancy was on the train for three days.	True	False	We don't know.
2. Nancy wrote three letters on the train.	True	False	We don't know.
3. Nancy slept and ate on the train.	True	False	We don't know.
4. Nancy isn't glad to be back.	True	False	We don't know.
5. "All in all" means "in general."	True	False	We don't know.

GRAMMAR   More Irregular Verbs in the Past Tense

Base Form		Irregular Form
sleep	→	slept
read	→	read (pronounced like the color *red*)
write	→	wrote
sit	→	sat
speak	→	spoke
meet	→	met
do	→	did
make	→	made

READ   *Make logical complete sentences with the words in the boxes.*

	slept	some nice people on the train.
I	spoke to	very little.
The passengers	did	a few friends.
She	made	late in the mornings.
Nancy	met	Nancy.
They	read	letters.
	wrote	a book.

		write	a train?
	Nancy	read	with Nancy?
Did	the passengers	sit	alone?
	she	speak	a book?
	Betty	go	a letter?
		take	to people?

Yes,	she	did.
No,	they	didn't.

WRITE   *Review the past tense of the verb **to be**. Fill in the spaces with **was** or **were**.*

Betty: __*Were*__ you on a small train or a big train?

Nancy: I __*was*__ on a very big train.

Betty: _____ there a dining car?

Nancy: Yes, there _____. And there _____ sleeping and sightseeing cars, too.

Betty: _____ there many people on the train?

Nancy: Yes, there _____ a lot of people.

Betty: _____ there many kids?

Nancy: No, there _____n't many kids. There _____ only about ten.

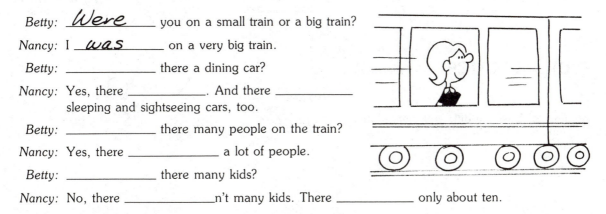

READ

This is Nancy's diary.

SATURDAY
· left New York
· read a book
· met Mr. and Mrs. Evans

SUNDAY
· slept late
· wrote letters
· ate dinner with the Evans's

MONDAY
· sat in sightseeing car
· saw beautiful scenery
· had lunch with a woman friend

TUESDAY
· got up early
· began new book

WEDNESDAY
· arrived in Los Angeles

PAIR PRACTICE   *Talk with another student about the diary above.*

Student 1: What did Nancy do ....?
Student 2: She ....

> WHAT DID NANCY DO THE FIRST DAY?

> SHE READ A BOOK.

PAIR PRACTICE   *Use the diary above.*

Student 1: When did Nancy ....?
Student 2: She ....

> WHEN DID NANCY READ A BOOK?

> SHE READ A BOOK ON THE FIRST DAY.

PAIR PRACTICE   *Use the diary above.*

Student 1: Did Nancy ....?
Student 2: Yes, she did. / No, she didn't.

> DID NANCY WRITE LETTERS ON THE LAST DAY?

> NO, SHE DIDN'T.

READ

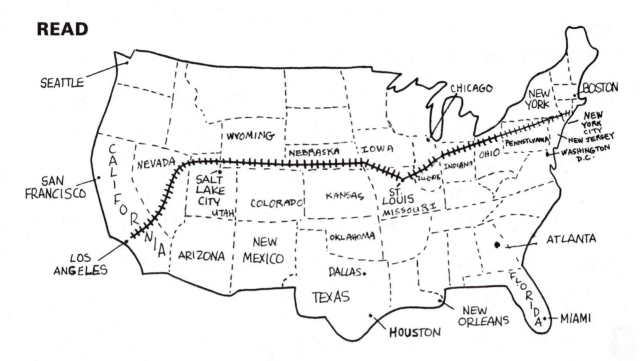

PAIR PRACTICE   *Talk with another student about the train route.*

Student 1: Did the train go through ....?
Student 2: Yes, it did. / No, it didn't.

PAIR PRACTICE   *Use the map above.*

Student 1: What states/cities did the train go through?
Student 2: It went through ....

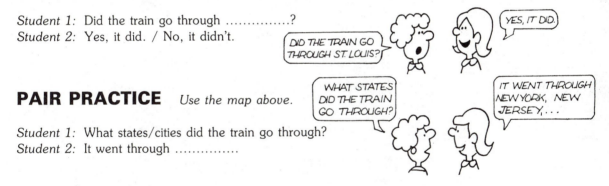

PAIR PRACTICE   *Use the phrases below. Answer in your own words.*

Student 1: What cities/states did you ....?
Student 2: I ....

1. visit
2. go to
3. see
4. drive through
5. live in
6. work in
7. write a letter to
8. get a letter from
9. leave
10. ....

CHALLENGE   *Fill in the missing names of the states in the map above.*

WRITE   *Fill in the spaces below with the words in the box.*

Betty is asking more questions about Nancy's train trip.

did	didn't	sleep	slept
write	wrote	meet	met

Betty: <u>*Did*</u> you <u>*sleep*</u> well on the train?

Nancy: I <u>*didn't sleep*</u> well the first night, but I <u>*slept*</u> very well after that.

Betty: _____ you _____ late every morning?

Nancy: Yes, I _____. And sometimes I _____ an hour in the afternoon, too.

Betty: _____ you _____ many letters?

Nancy: Yes, I _____ a few letters.

Betty: _____ you _____ postcards, too?

Nancy: No, I _____ _____ any postcards; I _____ all the postcards in New York.

Betty: How many people _____ you _____?

Nancy: I _____ a lot of people, but I _____ one especially nice couple the first day.

Betty: How _____ you _____ them?

Nancy: I _____ them in the dining car. We _____ for dinner every day after that.

WRITE   *Unscramble the words below the lines. All the words are the past tense of **to be** or irregular verbs.*

Dear Sis,

Thank you again for the dinner and the Broadway show. I _had_ a
                                                          dah

wonderful time. I'm glad I _____ the train back home. It _____ me
                          koto   vega

time to relax. I _____ a lot, I _____ a good book, and I _____
                 ptsle   dare   otwer

some letters. I _____ some interesting people and I _____ some
               tem   was

beautiful scenery.

I _____ lunch with my friend, Betty Fuller, yesterday. She asked
  adh

me a million questions about my trip. Maybe you know her. (I _____ whether
                                                            otfrog

you _____ her when you _____ here last year.) We _____ about my
    etm   erwe   ospek

trip and I _____ her a present. I _____ her a nice blouse in
           vgea   hgbuto

New York. (Do you remember when you _____ with me to buy it?) Betty
                                    tnew

_____ very surprised to get a present.
swa

Roy and the kids will be home soon, and dinner will be ready in a few minutes, so I have
to stop here.

Take care, and please write soon.

Love,
Nancy

PAIR PRACTICE   *Fold the page down the middle. Look only at your side. Do the exercise orally.*

Student 1	Student 2

Ask your partner questions with the words in the box below.

go	have	take	eat
drink	begin	get	buy
see	sit	forget	drive
leave	give	sleep	read
write	speak	meet	do

1. Where did you .... yesterday?
2. What did you .... yesterday?
3. What time did you .... yesterday?
4. How long did you .... yesterday?
5. Why did you .... yesterday?
6. When did you ....?
7. How did you ....?
8. Who did you ....?

Now answer your partner's questions with the time expressions in the box below.

every day	yesterday	tomorrow
sometimes	often	never
seldom	usually	always
last week	next week	every week
last month	next month	every month
last year	next year	every year
ago	in	on

Answer your partner's questions with the words in the box below.

went	had	took	ate
drank	began	got	bought
saw	sat	forgot	drove
left	gave	slept	read
wrote	spoke	met	did

*Now ask your partner questions with **when**. Use the verbs in the box below.*

see	buy	go	drink
have	take	give	forget
eat	get	begin	sit
live	call	help	listen
wash	fix	cook	watch
look	visit	start	end

1. When did you ....?
2. When do you ....?
3. When will you ....?

FOLD HERE
FOLD HERE

WORD BUILDING   The Prefix *re-*

• *We use the prefix* **re-** *with verbs to mean* **again** *or* **to restore to a previous condition**.

EXAMPLES

1. paint   repaint   2. write   rewrite

3. wash   rewash   4. build   rebuild

WRITE   *Rewrite the following sentences. Use the prefix* **re-**.

1. Sami *painted* his car again. _Sami repainted his car._

2. Nancy *read* the book again. _____

3. Sami *told* her the story again. _____

4. The students *took* the test again. _____

5. Nancy *wrote* the letter again. _____

6. Miko *visited* the senior citizens again. _____

7. Nancy's sister *invited* her again. _____

WRITE   *Fill in the spaces with verbs beginning with* **re-**. *Pay special attention to irregular verbs.*

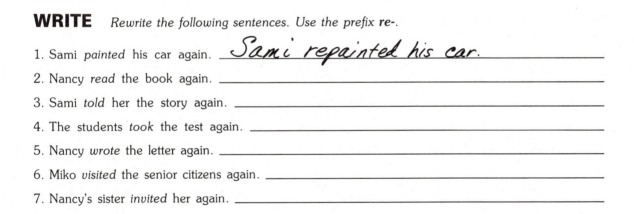

1. Roy wanted to *wash* the clothes again, so he ___*rewashed*___ them.

2. Jose didn't *make* his bed correctly the first time, so he _____ it.

3. Sami didn't *mix* the paint enough the first time, so he _____ it.

4. The students didn't *learn* the lesson the first time, so they _____ it.

5. They didn't *do* the exercise correctly the first time, so they _____ it.

8

THE PAST, PRESENT, AND FUTURE

- Review Chapter
- Test

LISTEN

Mr. Barns is introducing a newspaper reporter to Stephen Bratko.

WRITE   *Write short answers to the reporter's questions.*

1. Can I ask you a few questions?

2. Are you an ESL student?

3. Did you know English in your country?

4. Is it hard for you to learn English?

5. Do you practice outside of class?

6. Do you speak English at home?

7. Is English necessary for your work?

8. Is your English improving?

Sure, *you can.*

Yes, *I am.*

No, _____

Of course, _____

Yes, _____

No, _____

Yes, _____

Yes, _____

WRITE   *Fill in the spaces with the correct word.*

1. *Are*____ you married?

2. *Do*____ you have a wife and children?

3. _____ it difficult to begin a new life here?

4. _____ you have any relatives in this city?

5. _____ they help you at first?

6. _____ you working now?

7. _____ it easy to find a job?

8. _____ you stay in this country?

Yes, I am.

Yes, I do.

Yes, it was.

Yes, I do.

Yes, they did.

Yes, I am.

No, it wasn't.

Yes, I will.

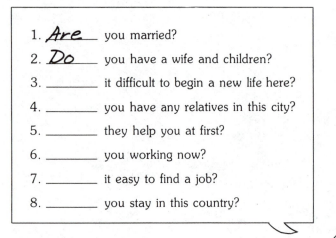

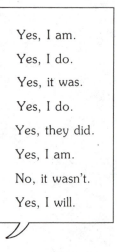

WRITE   *Help Stephen ask the reporter some questions, too. The answers will help you figure out the questions.*

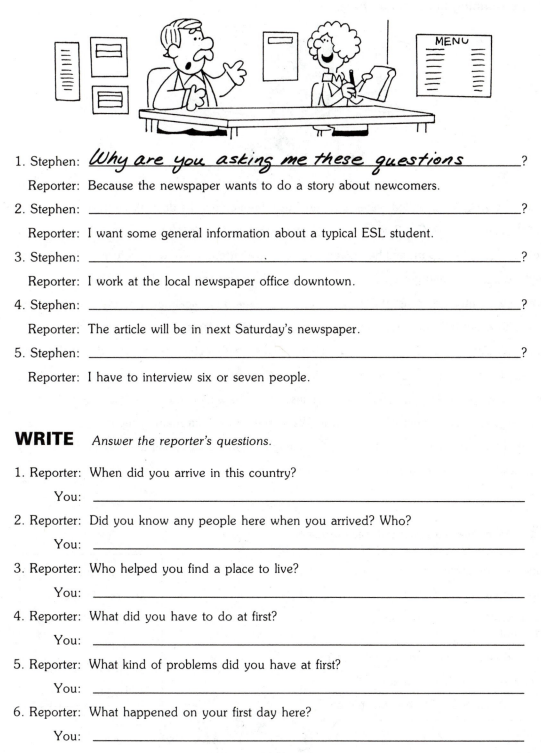

1. Stephen: *Why are you asking me these questions* ?

   Reporter: Because the newspaper wants to do a story about newcomers.

2. Stephen: _____?

   Reporter: I want some general information about a typical ESL student.

3. Stephen: _____?

   Reporter: I work at the local newspaper office downtown.

4. Stephen: _____?

   Reporter: The article will be in next Saturday's newspaper.

5. Stephen: _____?

   Reporter: I have to interview six or seven people.

WRITE   *Answer the reporter's questions.*

1. Reporter: When did you arrive in this country?

   You: _____

2. Reporter: Did you know any people here when you arrived? Who?

   You: _____

3. Reporter: Who helped you find a place to live?

   You: _____

4. Reporter: What did you have to do at first?

   You: _____

5. Reporter: What kind of problems did you have at first?

   You: _____

6. Reporter: What happened on your first day here?

   You: _____

WRITE   *Fill in the spaces with the prepositions **in**, **on**, **to**, or **at**.*

Stephen is describing his first day here.

Our first day *in* the United States was very busy. I remember the date. We arrived *in* Los Angeles *on* April 6th *at* 7 o'clock _____ the morning. I think it was _____ a Thursday. My cousin met us _____ the airport, and he drove us _____ his apartment. We were very tired, so we went _____ bed _____ noon and got up _____ five _____ the afternoon. _____ the evening, some old friends from our country visited us. We were happy _____ see them again after so many years. They spoke _____ us about our new city. They told us many interesting facts—especially about the weather here. They said we arrived _____ a typical day. They said the weather changes very little during the year. It's cool _____ the morning and _____ night, but it's generally warm _____ the afternoon. It's hot _____ the summer and not very cold _____ the winter. It rains _____ the winter and _____ the spring. Beautiful weather comes _____ November when it's clear. We learned a lot from them. They left _____ 11:30 _____ night. Then, we went _____ bed _____ midnight. It was a very long and wonderful first day _____ our new home. I'll never forget that day.

WRITE   *Match the questions with their answers.*

1. When did you arrive?
2. Who met you at the airport?
3. How did you get to your cousin's apartment?
4. What did you and your friends talk about?
5. How was the weather on that day?
6. What time did you go to bed on that day?

a. A cousin.
b. The weather.
c. On April sixth.
d. Typical.
e. About midnight.
f. By car.

READ

Stephen is telling the reporter about the first six months.

APRIL	MAY	JUNE
– arrived in the U.S.A. – enrolled kids in school – stayed with cousin	– moved to an apartment – looked for a job – applied at many companies – enrolled in adult school	– got a job – went to summer school – took driving lessons
JULY	AUGUST	SEPTEMBER
– bought a car – Wanda learned to drive	– bought some furniture – visited San Francisco – Wanda began to work	– new semester began – got a small raise at work

PAIR PRACTICE   *Talk with another student. Use the calendar above.*

Student 1: What did Stephen and Wanda
do in ....?
Student 2: They ....

> WHAT DID STEPHEN AND WANDA DO IN APRIL?

> THEY ARRIVED IN THE U.S.A.

PAIR PRACTICE   *Use the calendar above.*

Student 1: When did ....?
Student 2: He/She/They ....

> WHEN DID STEPHEN GET A JOB?

> HE GOT A JOB IN JUNE.

READ

PAIR PRACTICE   *Talk with another student. Use the dialog above and the past tense of* **have to**: **had to**.

Student 1: What did you have to do when you arrived in this city?
Student 2: I had to ....

PAIR PRACTICE   *Use the dialog above.*

Student 1: Did you have to .... when you arrived here?
Student 2: Yes, I did. / No, I didn't.

WRITE   *What did you have to do your first few months here? Write a list below.*

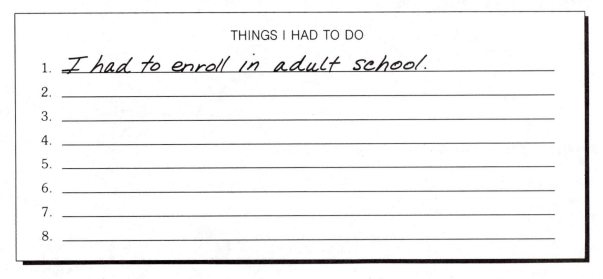

THINGS I HAD TO DO

1. *I had to enroll in adult school.*
2. _____
3. _____
4. _____
5. _____
6. _____
7. _____
8. _____

READ

Stephen is giving some advice.

Stephen: We were very lucky to have relatives here. It was nice to be with them again, and they helped me find a job. I was also lucky to meet some nice people here at school.
Reporter: Do you have any advice for newcomers?
Stephen: Yes, I do. Don't forget the past, enjoy the present, and plan for the future.

WRITE   *Help Stephen give some comments and advice for newcomers.*

1. It's hard to _begin a new life._
2. It's also hard to _____
3. It's expensive to _____
4. It's not very easy to _____
5. It's necessary to _____
6. It's important to _____
7. It's impossible to _____
8. It's interesting to _____
9. But it's possible to _____

READ

The reporter meets some of the ESL students.

PAIR PRACTICE *Talk with another student. Use the phrases above.*

Student 1: What will you do in the future?
Student 2: I'll ....
Student 1: What else?

WRITE *What will you and won't you do in the future? Make a list below.*

MY FUTURE PLANS

I will:	I won't:
1. _____	_____
2. _____	_____
3. _____	_____
4. _____	_____

WRITE   *Pretend you're a reporter and interview another student in your class. Ask the questions below. Then write the information.*

INTERVIEW QUESTIONS

1. Who are you interviewing? Name: _____

2. Where's he/she from? _____

3. Does he/she have friends or family here? Who? _____

_____

4. What's his/her occupation? _____

5. When did he/she arrive in this city? _____

6. Who helped him/her when he/she arrived? _____

7. Where does he/she live? _____

8. Does he/she work? _____

9. If he/she works, where? _____

10. How were his/her first few months? _____

11. What were his/her problems at first? _____

_____

12. What kind of advice does he/she have for newcomers? _____

_____

_____

13. What will he/she do in the future? _____

_____

_____

14. What does he/she like about this city? _____

_____

15. What doesn't he/she like about this city? _____

_____

16. What does he/she miss about his or her country? _____

_____

WRITE   *Write an article about the person you interviewed. Use the information from the previous page.*

_____ is an ESL student at _____

CHALLENGE   *Read the article to the students in your class.*

CHALLENGE   *Interview an English-speaking friend or neighbor. Write an article. Read it to the class.*

WRITE   *Fill out the crossword puzzle.*

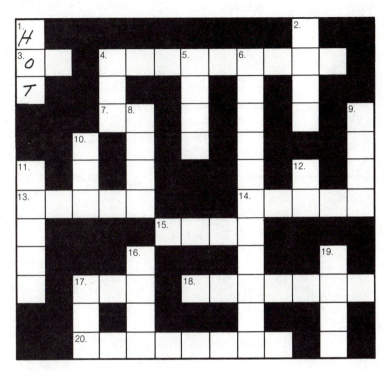

DOWN

1. Open the window because it's .... in here.

2. How .... does it cost?

4. A .... car usually uses a lot of gas.

5. Let's not buy a new car; let's buy a .... car.

6. Not expensive.

8. The ceiling is .... my head.

9. How .... people are there in this room?

10. She's not ....; she's very thin.

11. .... birthday!

12. Don't sit down; please stand ....

16. I work .... 8:00 a.m. to 5:00 p.m.

17. He lives very .... from here.

19. Please .... down. You're driving too fast.

ACROSS

3. It's dark in here. Please turn .... the light.

4. It's a .... day today!

7. I .... to school every day.

13. I usually go home .... work.

14. Please give me more water; this glass is ....

15. Please sit ....

17. I bought this present .... you.

18. This machine isn't noisy. It runs very ....

20. I'm sorry, but I don't .... your last name. I forgot it.

TEST   *Circle the correct answer.*

1. What floor is the office _____?
   a. in   c. to
   b. on   d. at

2. Raymond Monte lives in Los Angeles; he
   _____ in Santa Monica.
   a. live   c. doesn't lives
   b. don't live   d. doesn't live

3. Do Roberto and Raymond live together?
   No, _____.
   a. he doesn't   c. they doesn't
   b. he don't   d. they don't

4. That's Mr. Barns. He's my teacher. The
   students like _____ very much.
   a. her   c. his
   b. him   d. he's

5. How _____ do you work overtime?
   a. often   c. never
   b. always   d. sometimes

6. I take a bus _____.
   a. twice day   c. twice in a day
   b. twice a day   d. twice in day

7. It's hard _____ a good job.
   a. find   c. to find
   b. to finding   d. for find

8. The young man isn't _____ to work here.
   a. old enough   c. too old enough
   b. enough old   d. to young

9. If you want to go to college, you _____
   to study hard.
   a. must   c. have
   b. mustn't   d. has

10. Before you leave, you _____ take out the
    garbage.
    a. has   c. must
    b. have   d. must to

11. He can't go to college _____ good
    grades.
    a. with not   c. not have
    b. without   d. if not

12. I _____ to work on Sunday.
    a. don't must   c. don't have
    b. not must   d. doesn't have

13. Nancy and her daughter _____ shopping
    tomorrow.
    a. will goes   c. will to goes
    b. will to go   d. will go

14. What _____ you do tomorrow?
    a. are   c. will not
    b. will   d. were

15. How old _____ you?
    a. have   c. is
    b. has   d. are

16. Nancy will go to New York _____ bus.
    a. at   c. by
    b. with   d. in

17. When's the picnic _____ be?
    a. going   c. will
    b. going to   d. go to

18. The students _____ to bring the food.
    a. will   c. is going
    b. won't   d. are going

19. Where _____ you yesterday?
    a. was   c. were
    b. where   d. wear

20. I _____ at the picnic because I was sick in
    bed with a cold.
    a. was   c. weren't
    b. were   d. wasn't

21. _____ was a robbery at the adult school
    last night.
    a. The   c. They
    b. There   d. Their

22. Sami _____ a few hours overtime last week.
    a. works   c. worked
    b. work   d. will work

23. When _____ Yoshi study in the United States?
    a. is   c. do
    b. will   d. are

24. What _____ yesterday?
    a. do you did   c. did you did
    b. did you do   d. do you do

25. Where _____ before you moved here?
    a. did you live   c. did you lived
    b. lived you   d. do you live

26. When I moved here, I _____ to learn English quickly.
    a. tried   c. tryed
    b. tryd   d. treid

27. When Nancy was in New York, her sister _____ her some tickets.
    a. will buy   c. buyed
    b. bought   d. buys

28. Nancy Barns _____ to New York last month.
    a. go   c. was go
    b. went   d. goes

29. Did you _____ a taxi to the theater?
    a. taked   c. take
    b. tooked   d. took

30. Did you drink French champagne? No, we _____ French champagne.
    a. not drink   c. didn't drink
    b. not drank   d. didn't drank

31. Did you have a good time there? Yes, _____.
    a. I do   c. I have
    b. I did   d. I has

32. Did the train go _____ St. Louis?
    a. at   c. between
    b. through   d. across

33. How many people did you _____ on the train?
    a. meet   c. meeted
    b. met   d. meat

34. Nancy _____ some letters on the train.
    a. write   c. writed
    b. wrote   d. writing

35. What will you do _____?
    a. tomorrow   c. next day
    b. yesterday   d. last week

36. When did you return? I returned two _____.
    a. days ago   c. ago days
    b. days before   d. days past

37. I'll fix the sink _____.
    a. a week ago   c. next week
    b. last week   d. next day

38. Did Sami paint his car again? Yes, he _____ it yesterday.
    a. repainted   c. repaint
    b. paint   d. will paint

39. Do you plan to stay here? Yes, _____.
    a. I do   c. I did
    b. I am   d. I have

40. Is your English improving? Yes, _____.
    a. it is   c. it will
    b. I am   d. I will

PLEASE FOLLOW THE DIRECTIONS CAREFULLY

COMPETENCIES	• Understanding Written Directions
GRAMMAR	• More Regular Verbs in the Past Tense
VOCABULARY	• Commonly Used Technical Words
WORD BUILDING	• The Suffix *-al*

LISTEN

Joanne Yates is visiting Rita Landry.

Rita: Come in.

Joanne: What's up?

Rita: I bought two bookcases yesterday, but there's a problem.

Joanne: What's the problem?

Rita: They're unassembled, and I don't know if I can put them together. I'm not very good with tools.

Joanne: Maybe I can help. Where are the instructions?

Rita: Here they are.

INSTRUCTIONS TO ASSEMBLE BOOKCASE

Tools needed: screwdriver and hammer.
Follow the steps below carefully.

1. Remove the pieces from the box.
2. Make sure all pieces are included.
   This kit includes screws, nails, and seven
   pieces of wood: top board, bottom board,
   two side boards, back board, and two shelves.
3. Place all pieces on the floor.
4. Position the sides and match the letters
   on the ends of the boards. (See picture.)
5. Place screws in the holes and attach sides.
6. Tighten all screws.
7. Nail the large board to the back side of the
   bookcase.
8. Lift bookcase upright.
9. Insert and adjust shelves.

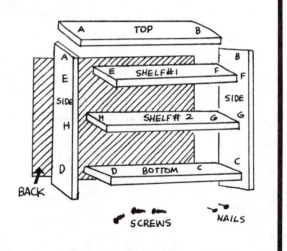

UNDERSTAND   *Circle **True, False,** or **We don't know.***

1. "What's up?" means "What are you doing?"	True	False	We don't know.
2. "Assemble" means "put together."	True	False	We don't know.
3. "Make sure" means "check."	True	False	We don't know.
4. Joanne doesn't want to help Rita.	True	False	We don't know.
5. They need tools to assemble the bookcase.	True	False	We don't know.

GRAMMAR   More Regular Verbs in the Past Tense

- *Most common verbs in English are irregular, but most other verbs are **regular**. To form the past tense, simply add the **-d** or **-ed** ending. (See Chapter 6.)*

EXAMPLES	*Present Tense*	*Past Tense*
	remove	remove<u>d</u>
	check	check<u>ed</u>
	place	place<u>d</u>

READ

1. Remove pieces from box.

2. Check all parts.

3. Place pieces on the floor.

4. Position pieces.

5. Place screws in the holes.

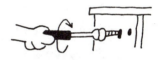

6. Tighten screws.

7. Nail large board to the back of the bookcase.

8. Lift bookcase upright.

9. Insert and adjust shelves.

PAIR PRACTICE   *Talk about how Rita and Joanne assembled the bookcase. Use the past tense.*

Student 1: What a beautiful bookcase! What did they do to make it?
Student 2: First, they ....
Student 1: What did they do next?
Student 2: Next they ....

WRITE   *Fill in the spaces below with the past tense of the verbs in the box.*

follow	adjust	nail	attach
include	position	remove	check
place	tighten	insert	lift

Joanne and Rita are looking at one of the assembled bookcases.

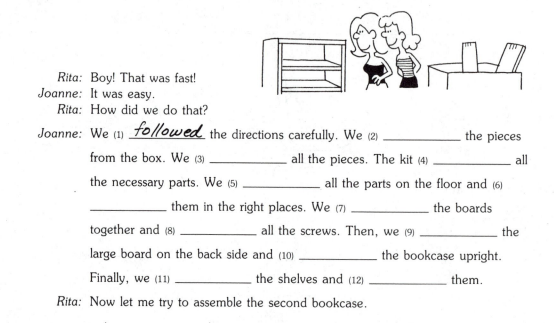

Rita: Boy! That was fast!

Joanne: It was easy.

Rita: How did we do that?

Joanne: We (1) *followed* the directions carefully. We (2) _____ the pieces from the box. We (3) _____ all the pieces. The kit (4) _____ all the necessary parts. We (5) _____ all the parts on the floor and (6) _____ them in the right places. We (7) _____ the boards together and (8) _____ all the screws. Then, we (9) _____ the large board on the back side and (10) _____ the bookcase upright. Finally, we (11) _____ the shelves and (12) _____ them.

Rita: Now let me try to assemble the second bookcase.

WRITE   *Help Rita. Label the pieces for her. Use the words in the box.*

bottom shelf	shelf	side	back
top shelf	nails	screws	box

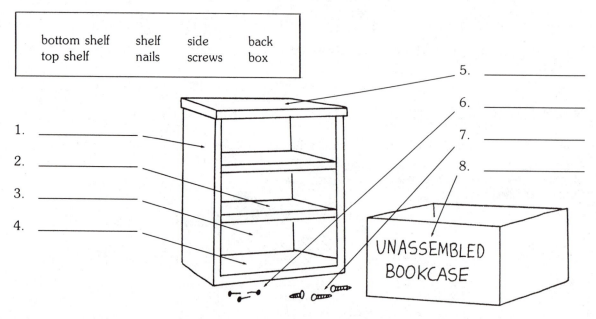

1. _____

2. _____

3. _____

4. _____

5. _____

6. _____

7. _____

8. _____

UNASSEMBLED BOOKCASE

LISTEN

Rita has another problem.

> IT WORKS.

> IT WAS ONLY A BURNED-OUT BULB.

      Rita: Before you go, can you help me check my living room lamp? It doesn't
            work.
    Joanne: Did you check the light bulb?
      Rita: No, I didn't. I don't like to work with electrical equipment.
    Joanne: Let's begin with the light bulb.
            First, let's turn off the lamp.
            OK. Now unplug the cord.
            Remove the lamp shade.
            Unscrew the light bulb. Check the bulb.
            Get a new bulb. Is the old one burned out?
      Rita: Yes, it is.
    Joanne: Screw the new bulb in the socket.
            Place the shade back on the lamp.
            Plug the cord in the outlet.
            Now turn on the switch.
      Rita: It works!
    Joanne: It was only a burned-out bulb. Here. You can throw it away.
      Rita: That looks very easy.
    Joanne: It is. You can do it yourself next time.

UNDERSTAND   *Circle **True**, **False**, or **We don't know**.*

1. Rita fixed the lamp.	True	False	We don't know.
2. The living room lamp had a broken plug.	True	False	We don't know.
3. The living room lamp had a burned-out bulb.	True	False	We don't know.
4. Joanne is an electrician.	True	False	We don't know.
5. Joanne likes to fix things.	True	False	We don't know.

READ

1. Turn off the lamp.

2. Unplug the cord.

3. Remove the shade.

4. Unscrew the bulb.

5. Get a new bulb.

6. Screw in the new bulb.

7. Place the shade back on the lamp.

8. Plug in the cord.

9. Turn on the switch.

PAIR PRACTICE   *Talk about what Joanne did. Use the past tense.*

Student 1: What did Joanne do first?
Student 2: She ....
Student 1: Then what did she do?
Student 2: Then she ....

PAIR PRACTICE   *Use **had to** or **didn't have to** in the answers.*

Student 1: Did she have to ....?
Student 2: Yes, she had to .... it.
                              or
            No, she didn't have to .... it.

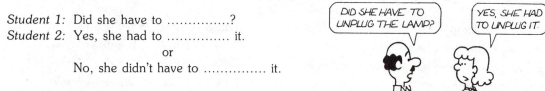

WRITE   *Fill in the spaces below with the past tense of the verbs in the box.*

turn on	get	screw	turn off
remove	plug	unscrew	check
place	unplug		

Rita is trying to repeat the directions.

Rita: Let me see if I can repeat that. First, you (1)*turned off* the lamp. Then,

you (2)_____ the cord. You (3)_____ the shade, and

(4)_____ the light bulb. You (5)_____ the bulb, and it was

burned out. You (6)_____ a new bulb, (7)_____ it in,

(8)_____ the shade back on the lamp, (9)_____ the cord in the

outlet, and (10)_____ the lamp. Right?

Joanne: That's right. Next time, you can replace a burned-out bulb.
Rita: What's the name of this thing again?
Joanne: That's a plug.

WRITE   *Help Rita learn the names of the parts. Match the words in the box with the pictures.*

plug	switch	socket
cord	outlet	light bulb

THIS IS....

1. _____   2. _____

3. _____   4. _____

5. _____   6. _____

WRITE   *Write sentences about what Joanne is doing.*

1. *She's turning on the lamp.*

2. _____

3. _____

4. _____

5. _____

6. _____

CHALLENGE   *Put the pictures above in the correct order.*

WRITE   *Fill in the spaces below with the words in the box.*

replace	turn on	turn off	throw away
remove	close	open	

Now Rita is replacing a dirty filter in the heater.

Let me see. Where do I begin?

1. First, I *turn off* the heater.

2. Then, I have to _____ the heater cover.

3. I _____ the dirty filter.

4. I _____ it with the new filter.

5. I have to _____ the cover.

6. Then I _____ _____ the heater.

7. And I _____ _____ the dirty filter.

CHALLENGE   *How many machines and appliances can you name that use electrical plugs?*

LISTEN

A man is asking Rita for help at the supermarket.

Man: Excuse me, ma'am, can you help me use this machine? I have to make a photocopy of this paper.

Rita: Sure, let me read the instructions to you.

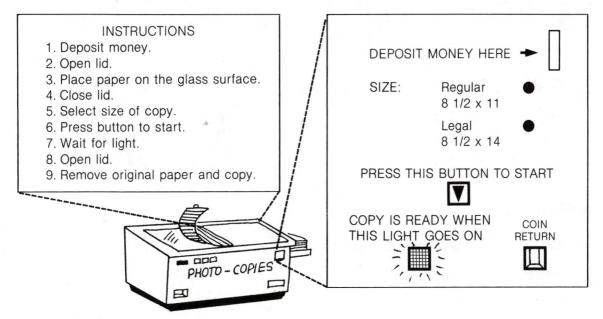

INSTRUCTIONS
1. Deposit money.
2. Open lid.
3. Place paper on the glass surface.
4. Close lid.
5. Select size of copy.
6. Press button to start.
7. Wait for light.
8. Open lid.
9. Remove original paper and copy.

DEPOSIT MONEY HERE ➡

SIZE: Regular   ●
         8 1/2 x 11

         Legal   ●
         8 1/2 x 14

PRESS THIS BUTTON TO START
▼

COPY IS READY WHEN
THIS LIGHT GOES ON   COIN
                            RETURN

UNDERSTAND   *Circle **True**, **False**, or **We don't know**.*

1. The man knows how to use the machine.   True   False   We don't know.
2. "Select" means "choose."   True   False   We don't know.
3. A copy costs ten cents.   True   False   We don't know.
4. "Legal size" means "a small size."   True   False   We don't know.
5. A page from this book is legal size.   True   False   We don't know.

READ

1. Deposit money.

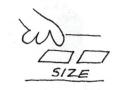

2. Open lid.

3. Place paper on glass surface.

4. Close lid.

SIZE

5. Select size.

RRRRR

6. Press button to start.

RRR

7. Wait for light.

8. Open lid.

9. Remove original and copy.

PAIR PRACTICE   *Talk about the pictures above. Use the present continuous tense.*

Student 1: What is Rita doing?
Student 2: She's .... the money.

WHAT IS RITA DOING?

SHE'S DEPOSITING THE MONEY.

WRITE   *Explain Rita's steps above. Use the past tense.*

1. *First, she deposited the money.*
2. _____
3. _____
4. _____
5. _____
6. _____
7. _____
8. _____
9. _____

READ   *Put the instructions below in the correct order.*

TO OPERATE COFFEE MACHINE:

_____ Lift plastic door.

_____ Press button to start.

___*1*___ Deposit money.

_____ Remove cup.

_____ Select item.

TO OPERATE MICROWAVE OVEN:

_____ Remove hot food.

_____ Close door.

_____ Press button to start.

_____ Wait for red light telling that food is cooked.

_____ Place cold food in oven.

___*1*___ Open door.

_____ Select time and temperature.

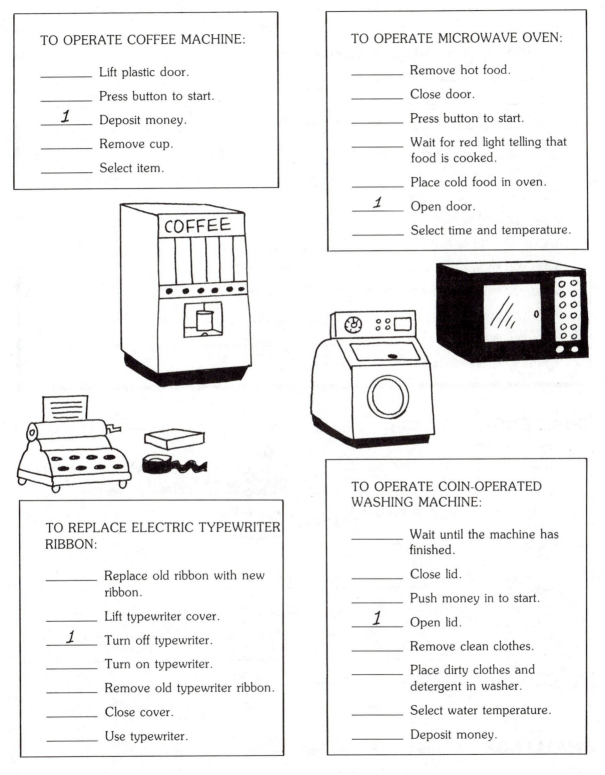

TO REPLACE ELECTRIC TYPEWRITER RIBBON:

_____ Replace old ribbon with new ribbon.

_____ Lift typewriter cover.

___*1*___ Turn off typewriter.

_____ Turn on typewriter.

_____ Remove old typewriter ribbon.

_____ Close cover.

_____ Use typewriter.

TO OPERATE COIN-OPERATED WASHING MACHINE:

_____ Wait until the machine has finished.

_____ Close lid.

_____ Push money in to start.

___*1*___ Open lid.

_____ Remove clean clothes.

_____ Place dirty clothes and detergent in washer.

_____ Select water temperature.

_____ Deposit money.

WRITE   *Fill out the questionnaire.*

QUESTIONNAIRE

1. What kind of machines can you operate?

   a. _____   b. _____

   c. _____   d. _____

   e. _____   f. _____

   g. _____   h. _____

2. What kind of tools can you use? _____

   _____

3. Can you follow directions correctly? _____

4. Can you lift heavy boxes? _____

5. Do you know how to work with electrical equipment? _____

6. Do you have any mechanical skills? _____

7. Do you like to build things? _____

8. Do you like to fix things? _____

9. Who fixes broken things in your home? _____

CHALLENGE   *Explain how to play a record on a record player. Use some of the words in the box.*

RECORD   ARM   NEEDLE   TURNTABLE

place
turn on
position
lift
select
listen to
needle
record
record player
replace
arm
music
turntable

1. _____

2. _____

3. _____

4. _____

5. _____

6. _____

CHALLENGE   *Read the directions you wrote above to the students in class.*

PAIR PRACTICE   *Fold the page down the middle. Look only at your side. Do the exercise orally.*

Student 1	Student 2

Student 1

Listen to the questions from your partner and find the answers in the picture below.

Now ask your partner these questions.

1. Is there a lamp in your picture?
2. Where is it?
3. Does the lamp have a plug?
4. Is the plug in an outlet?
5. What is next to the lamp?
6. Is there a bulb in the lamp?
7. Is the light bulb burned out?
8. Where is the lamp shade?
9. Is there anything else in the picture?

Student 2

Ask your partner these questions.

1. Is there a bookcase in the picture?
2. What's on the top of it?
3. What's on the bottom shelf?
4. What's inside it?
5. What's on the left side of it?
6. What's on the middle shelf?
7. Is there a plant in the picture?
8. What else is in the picture?
9. What is it?

Listen to the questions from your partner and find the answers in the picture below.

FOLD HERE

WORD BUILDING   The Suffix *-al*

- *We can form adjectives by adding the suffix **-al** to many nouns.*

EXAMPLES

1. A mechanic uses mechanical skills.
2. A dentist works on dental problems.

WRITE   *Make adjectives from the following nouns.*

1. nation   _____
2. practice   _____
3. origin   _____

4. instrument   _____
5. magic   _____
6. classic   _____

WRITE   *Fill in the spaces with adjectives ending in the suffix **-al**.*

1. A *technician* has *technical* skills.

2. A *politician* works with _____ problems.

3. A *person* can have many _____ problems.

4. *Musicians* usually have _____ skills.

5. An *electrician* usually knows about _____ problems.

WRITE   *Write original sentences with the following adjectives.*

1. physical   _____
2. special   _____
3. general   _____
4. official   _____
5. medical   _____

10

ISN'T THAT WOMEN'S WORK?

COMPETENCIES	• Identifying Daily Activities • Making a Household Work Schedule
GRAMMAR	• Expressions with *do, make,* and *get*
VOCABULARY	• Household Chores • Daily Activities
WORD BUILDING	• The Suffix *-ing* Used as a Noun (Gerund)
SPELLING	• Rules for Adding *-ing* to a Verb

LISTEN

It's Saturday morning and Roy Barns is vacuuming. The door bell rings. James Fuller is at the door.

James: Are you ready for our tennis game?

Roy: I'll be ready in a minute.

James: What are you doing?

Roy: I'm doing some housework. Let me turn off this vacuum cleaner. I can't hear you. It makes too much noise.

James: Isn't that women's work?

Roy: We all share the housework in this family. Nancy does the laundry, the ironing, and the bathrooms. I do the gardening, and the kids help me with the cleaning. I do the vacuuming and the windows, and Patty does the dusting and the dishes. Bobby helps, too. The kids do a pretty good job. They even make their beds.

James: Who does the shopping?

Roy: We all do the shopping on Friday.

James: And the cooking? Who does that?

Roy: Nancy and I both do. I usually make breakfast and she makes dinner. She doesn't let me make dinner. She says I make a mess in the kitchen. We sometimes let Patty make a meal, but we make sure one of us is in the kitchen with her. What do you do, Jim? Don't you help your wife do any housework?

James: Well, oh, ah, hum, let's play tennis.

Roy: Oh, I see.

UNDERSTAND   *Circle **True**, **False**, or **We don't know**.*

1. Roy likes to do housework.	True	False	We don't know.
2. Nancy does the gardening.	True	False	We don't know.
3. The family does the shopping together.	True	False	We don't know.
4. James Fuller helps his wife do housework.	True	False	We don't know.
5. "Even" means "also."	True	False	We don't know.
6. "I see" means "I understand."	True	False	We don't know.

GRAMMAR   *do* and *make*

- *We often use expressions with* **do** *and* **make** *to describe household duties.* **Do** *means perform an activity.* **Make** *usually means produce something.*

  EXAMPLES

Expressions with do		*Meaning*	*Expressions with* do		*Meaning*
do the housework	=	work in the house	do the shopping	=	shop for food
do the dishes	=	wash the dishes	do the cleaning	=	clean the house
do the cooking	=	cook	do the dusting	=	dust the furniture
do the work	=	work	do the vacuuming	=	vacuum the carpets and floors
do a good job	=	work well			
do the laundry	=	wash and dry clothes	do the gardening	=	work in the yard
do the ironing	=	iron the clothes	do the windows	=	clean the windows
do the bathrooms	=	clean the bathrooms	do nothing	=	perform no work

Expressions with make		Meaning
make the beds	=	arrange the bedding (sheets, blankets, pillows)
make the meals	=	prepare/cook food or meals (breakfast, lunch, dinner)
make a mess	=	create a mess
make noise	=	produce noise
make a mistake	=	do incorrectly
make sure	=	check

READ   *Make logical complete sentences with the words in the boxes.*

Roy		the housework.
Nancy		the vacuuming.
Patty	do	the shopping.
The family	does	the cooking.
The kids	make	their beds.
The vacuum cleaner	makes	breakfast.
They		noise.
I		laundry and ironing.

	Roy		breakfast?		
	Nancy		noise?		
Do	Patty	do	the dusting?		
	the family		a good job?		
Does	the vacuum	make	the gardening?		
	they		bathrooms?		
	you		dishes?		

	I	
Yes,	he	do.
	she	
No,	it	does.
	they	

WRITE   *Match the questions with their answers.*

1. Who does the dusting?
2. Who does the cooking?
3. Who does the bathrooms?
4. Who does the shopping?
5. Who does the dishes?
6. Who does the laundry?
7. Who does the gardening?
8. Who does the windows?

a. I wash the windows.
b. Nancy washes the clothes.
c. Patty dusts the furniture.
d. I work in the yard.
e. Patty washes them after we eat.
f. We all buy the food.
g. Nancy and I make the meals.
h. Nancy scrubs the bathtub.

WRITE   *Match the questions with their answers.*

1. Who makes the beds?
2. Who makes dinner?
3. Who makes breakfast?
4. What makes noise?
5. Who makes mistakes?
6. Who makes a mess?
7. Who makes sure Patty's OK in the kitchen?

a. Nancy cooks the evening meal.
b. I prepare the morning meal.
c. Nancy or I check on her.
d. The vacuum is loud.
e. I'm always neat and clean.
f. The kids straighten the sheets, blankets, and pillows.
g. I never do anything wrong.

READ

```
HOUSEHOLD RESPONSIBILITES
```

	LAST SATURDAY	THIS SATURDAY
NANCY	DINNER LAUNDRY IRONING	DINNER BATHROOMS
ROY	BREAKFAST GARDENING	BREAKFAST VACUUMING WINDOWS
PATTY	LUNCH BEDS DISHES	DUSTING CAKE DISHES

PAIR PRACTICE

Talk with another student about the chart above. Use the present habitual tense.

Student 1: Who does/makes ....?
Student 2: .... does/makes ....

WHO DOES THE DUSTING?

PATTY DOES THE DUSTING.

PAIR PRACTICE

Talk about the chart above. Use the past tense.

Student 1: Who did/made .... this/last Saturday?
Student 2: .... did/made ....

PATTY MADE LUNCH LAST SATURDAY.

WHO MADE LUNCH LAST SATURDAY?

PAIR PRACTICE

Talk about the chart above. Use the future tense.

Student 1: When will .... do/make ....?
Student 2: .... will do/make ....

SHE WILL MAKE A CAKE ON SATURDAY.

WHEN WILL PATTY MAKE A CAKE?

PAIR PRACTICE   *Talk with another student. Use the words below.*

Student 1: Who does/makes .... in your family?
Student 2: .... do/does/make/makes ....

1. the cooking
2. the laundry
3. dinner
4. ironing
5. housework
6. cleaning
7. vacuuming
8. breakfast
9. the dishes
10. shopping
11. noise
12. mess

WHO DOES THE COOKING IN YOUR FAMILY?

I DO THE COOKING.

PAIR PRACTICE   *Use the words below.*

Student 1: Do you know how to do/make ....?
Student 2: Yes, I do. / No, I don't.

1. coffee
2. a cake
3. the beds
4. the dishes
5. the ironing
6. the laundry
7. the bathroom
8. the cooking
9. the gardening
10. a good meal
11. a good job
12. ....

DO YOU KNOW HOW TO MAKE COFFEE?

YES, I DO.

WRITE   *List your personal or family household responsibilities below. Use expressions with **do** and **make**.*

WEEKLY HOUSEHOLD RESPONSIBILITIES

Duties

Name: _____

1. _____
2. _____
3. _____

Name: _____

1. _____
2. _____
3. _____

Name: _____

1. _____
2. _____
3. _____

WRITE   *Replace the phrases under the lines with expressions from the box. Change the verbs to the past tense.*

do the gardening	make a mess	do the dishes	do the bathroom
do the shopping	do the laundry	do the cleaning	do the cooking
do a good job	do the work	do the housework	do the ironing

Roy and James are playing tennis.

Roy: Who (1) *did the housework* _____ in your home when you were a child?
worked in the house

James: My mom and three sisters (2)_____, and they (3)_____, too.
worked   worked well

My mother (4)_____ and (5)_____, too. My big sister,
cooked   shopped for food

Susan, (6)_____ and she also (7)_____.
washed the clothes   ironed the clothes

My sister Pauline (8)_____ and (9)_____.
cleaned the house   cleaned the bathrooms

My little sister, Rina, (10)_____.
washed the dishes

Roy: What did you do?

James: I (11) _____ with my dad.
worked in the yard

Roy: Is that all?

James: No, I often (12) _____, too!
created a mess

DISCUSSION   *Discuss the following questions in class.*

1. Is it OK for men to do housework? Why or why not?
2. Do the men do housework in your home? What kind?
3. How much time do you spend doing housework every week?
4. How many hours did your mother spend doing housework when you were a child? Why?
5. Why did women stay home and do housework in the past?
6. Why do many women work outside the home today?
7. Are there different occupations for men and women? Why or why not?
8. What is "women's work" and what is "men's work" in your culture?
9. Do men and women get the same pay for the same kind of work? Why or why not?
10. Are men and women equal? Why or why not?

LISTEN

Roy and James are returning from their tennis game.

Roy: My hands are full. Can you get the door for me?
James: Sure.
Roy: Let's sit down. I'll get us some cold drinks. I really get thirsty and a little tired after a tennis game with you.
James: Sorry, but I can't stay. I have to go.* I have to do a lot of things today. I have to get a haircut, get some money from the automatic money machine at the bank, get some new shoes, get the mail, and get ready for a dinner party tonight.

The telephone rings. Nancy answers it.

(A minute later.)

Nancy: James, it was for you. It was your wife.
James: What did she want?
Nancy: She wants you to get home.

UNDERSTAND   *Circle **True**, **False**, or **We don't know**.*

1. Roy has to do a lot of things today.	True	False	We don't know.
2. Roy is tired.	True	False	We don't know.
3. James is thirsty.	True	False	We don't know.
4. James can stay at Roy's house.	True	False	We don't know.
5. James's wife wants him to come home.	True	False	We don't know.

---

* A popular variation of **have to** is **have got to**, usually pronounced **'v gotta**.

GRAMMAR   *get*

- *The verb* **get** *has many different meanings.*
- *The past tense is irregular:* **got**.

EXAMPLES

Expressions with get		*Meaning*
get the door or telephone	=	open the door/answer the telephone
get a cold drink (or object)	=	go, pick up, and return with it
get tired, thirsty	=	become tired, thirsty
get a haircut	=	when a person cuts your hair
get money (or an object)	=	receive money
get some shoes (or object)	=	buy some shoes
get the mail	=	open a mailbox and take the mail
get ready for a party (or event)	=	prepare for a party
get home/get to a place	=	come home/arrive at a place
get up	=	rise (usually in the morning)
get dressed	=	put on clothes

READ   *Make logical complete sentences with the words in the box.*

Nancy	got	the mail	soon.
Roy	will get	a haircut	every day.
James	get	a check	in the afternoon.
I	gets	home	yesterday.
		ready for work	in the morning.
		food	at 10 p.m.
		hungry	on Saturday.
		up	every month.
		dressed	

WRITE   *Match the questions with their answers.*

1. When will you get a haircut?
2. Can I get you some juice?
3. What will you get at the store?
4. When will you get home?
5. What kind of mail do you get?
6. Are you getting thirsty?

a. I'll buy some shoes.

b. I don't receive many letters; I receive bills.

c. The barber will cut my hair at 2 o'clock.

d. No, I'm not, but I'm getting a little hungry.

e. I'll arrive at about 4 p.m.

f. No, thanks. I'm not thirsty.

PAIR PRACTICE

*Talk with another student about the pictures below. Use **get** in the present continuous.*

Student 1: What's he/she doing?
Student 2: He/She's ....

PAIR PRACTICE

*Use **become** in the question and **get** in the answer. Use the words below, and answer in your own words.*

Student 1: When do you usually become ....?
Student 2: I usually get ....

1. tired
2. thirsty
3. hungry
4. nervous
5. sleepy

6. sick
7. angry
8. hot
9. cold
10. ....

PAIR PRACTICE

*Use **bring** in the question and **get** in the answer.*

Student 1: Can you bring me ....?
Student 2: Sure, I'll get you a .... right away.

1. a cold drink
2. some coffee
3. a sandwich
4. a chair
5. some food

6. a magazine
7. some water
8. a pillow
9. ....

PAIR PRACTICE   *Use **get** in the question. Use **buy** and the phrases below in the answer.*

Student 1: What did you get?
Student 2: I bought ....

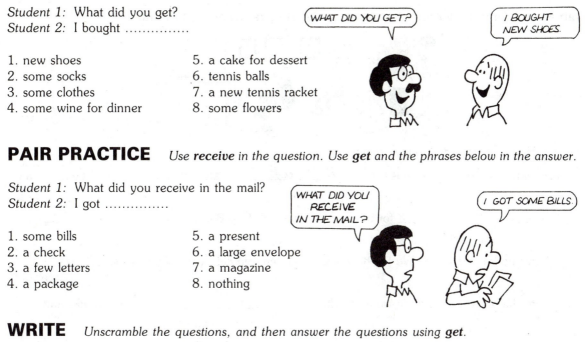

1. new shoes
2. some socks
3. some clothes
4. some wine for dinner
5. a cake for dessert
6. tennis balls
7. a new tennis racket
8. some flowers

PAIR PRACTICE   *Use **receive** in the question. Use **get** and the phrases below in the answer.*

Student 1: What did you receive in the mail?
Student 2: I got ....

1. some bills
2. a check
3. a few letters
4. a package
5. a present
6. a large envelope
7. a magazine
8. nothing

WRITE   *Unscramble the questions, and then answer the questions using **get**.*

QUESTIONNAIRE

1. you/get/when/they visit you/your guests/do/What/?

   Question: *What do you get your guests when they visit you?*

   Answer: _____

2. get/Do/enough money/your bills/you/to pay/?

   Question: _____

   Answer: _____

3. sick/you/How often/do/get/?

   Question: _____

   Answer: _____

4. to work/What time/you/get/or school/do/?

   Question: _____

   Answer: _____

5. at the supermarket/What/get/you/do/every week/usually/?

   Question: _____

   Answer: _____

WRITE   *Replace the words under the lines with expressions using **get**. Make sure that the verbs are in the past tense.*

James and Betty Fuller are at a dinner party. They're speaking to a guest.

Guest: How was your day today, James?

James: Don't ask. It was very busy. I (1)_____*got up*_____ late this morning. I had breakfast and
                                                       rose*

(2)_____ for my tennis game with Roy Barns. I (3)_____ to
       prepare   went

his house at 10 a.m. We left his place about ten minutes later. When we (4)_____
                                                             came

to the tennis courts, they were all full, so we (5)_____ some drinks and
                                                bought

waited for an empty court. We played for two hours, then Roy wanted to stop because he

(6)_____. In the afternoon I went to the bank for some money, but I
      became tired

(7)_____ any because the automatic money machine was broken.
      didn't receive

Then, I went to the shoe store and (8)_____ some new shoes with my
                                       bought

credit card. After that, I walked to the barber and (9)_____. Then, I
                                                he cut my hair

drove to the post office and (10)_____. When I (11)_____,
                           picked up the mail   came home

I (12)_____ for this dinner party. We left the house and drove here. We
       prepared

(13)_____ here a few minutes ago. You (14)_____ us a
       came   brought*

drink and here we are.

Guest: Relax and have a good time. The night is young.

---

* **Rose** is the past tense of **rise**, and **brought** is the past tense of **bring**.

WRITE   *Write a story about last weekend. Describe what you did. Use some of the expressions in the box. Make sure you use the past tense.*

do the housework	do the dusting	make a mistake
do the cooking	do the vacuuming	make a mess
do the work	do a good job	make noise
do the dishes	do the gardening	get up
do the laundry	do the bathrooms	get ready for
do the ironing	make the beds	get home
do the shopping	make breakfast	get (buy)
do the cleaning	make dinner	get (receive)

LAST WEEKEND

_____

_____

_____

_____

_____

_____

_____

_____

_____

_____

_____

_____

_____

_____

_____

_____

_____

_____

CHALLENGE   *Read your story to the students in class.*

CHALLENGE   *Ask an English-speaking friend or neighbor about his/her past weekend. Write his/her story. Read it to the class.*

WORD BUILDING   The Suffix *-ing* Used as a Noun (Gerund)

- *We use the suffix **-ing** in the present continuous tense.*

EXAMPLE   I'm   reading   this sentence now.

- *We can also use words with the suffix **-ing** as nouns (gerunds).*

EXAMPLES

1. Buying food is necessary.
2. Swimming is fun.
3. Roy does the vacuuming.
4. They do the shopping together.
5. We like eating out at a restaurant.
6. She hates working.

SPELLING   Rules for Adding *-ing* to a Verb

- *When a verb ends in a consonant-vowel-consonant pattern and the final vowel is stressed, the last consonant is doubled before adding **-ing**. A final **w**, **x**, or **y** is never doubled.*

EXAMPLES   **Consonant Doubled**   **Not Doubled**

swim	→	swimming		show	→	showing
sit	→	sitting		fix	→	fixing
run	→	running		say	→	saying

WRITE   *Fill in the spaces below with your own words. Use gerunds.*

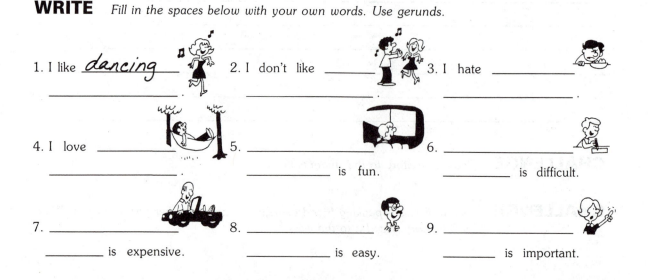

1. I like *dancing*
2. I don't like _____ .
3. I hate _____ .
4. I love _____ .
5. _____ is fun.
6. _____ is difficult.
7. _____ is expensive.
8. _____ is easy.
9. _____ is important.

11

EVERYTHING WENT WRONG

COMPETENCIES	• Describing a Series of Events
GRAMMAR	• Intransitive Verbs with Prepositions of Direction • Two-Word Verbs
VOCABULARY	• Common Separable and Non-Separable Two-Word Verbs
PRONUNCIATION	• The /ər/ Sound

LISTEN

Carmen Martinez is at a restaurant with her friend, George. She's describing her day.

George: How was your day, Carmen?

Carmen: Everything went wrong today! I woke up at eight-thirty and got up quickly because I was late for work. I took a shower, put on my work clothes, and went to the kitchen for a fast breakfast. I wasn't very careful, so I dropped a cup of coffee on the floor and made a big mess. I cleaned it up and threw away the broken pieces. Then, I went out of the house, and ran to the bus stop. I opened my handbag, looked for some money for a bus ticket, and took out some change, but it wasn't enough. I went back home, got some money, and ran back to the bus stop. I got on the bus, but it was the wrong bus, so I got off and walked to work. I got to work two hours late. When I arrived, I took off my coat, punched in, set up my equipment, turned on the machine, picked up my tools, and began to work. A few minutes later, I looked around and saw nobody. Finally, I turned off my machine, put down my tools, sat down, and remembered it was Saturday—my day off!

UNDERSTAND   *Circle True, False, or We don't know.*

1. Carmen works on Saturday.	True	False	We don't know.
2. The bus ticket costs fifty cents.	True	False	We don't know.
3. She drove to work.	True	False	We don't know.
4. She got to work on time.	True	False	We don't know.
5. "A day off" means "a day you don't have to work."	True	False	We don't know.

GRAMMAR   Intransitive Verbs with Prepositions of Direction

- *Here are some common prepositions:*

Prepositions	Meaning	Prepositions	Meaning
up		out	
down		in	
around		back	

- *We often use particles (words that look like prepositions) with intransitive verbs such as* **go**, **come**, **run**, **drive**, **look**, *and* **sit**.

EXAMPLES

Carmen	**woke**	**up**	at 8:30.
She	**got**	**up**	quickly.
She	**went**	**out**	of the house.
She	**went**	**back**	home.
She	**ran**	**back**	to the bus stop.
She	**looked**	**around.**	
She	**sat**	**down.**	

READ   *Make logical complete sentences with the words in the box.*

	went		to the bus stop.
	ran	around	home.
I	woke	up	the room.
	got	back	of the house.
Carmen	looked	down	early.
	sat	out	quickly.
	came		at 8:30.

READ   *Make logical questions with the words in the box. Then answer them.*

			get	back?
			wake	around?
When	do		sit	up?
Where	did	you	look	down?
What	will		come	out?
			run	

READ

1. wake up
2. get up
3. go out
4. go back home

5. run back to the bus stop
6. punch in
7. look around
8. sit down

PAIR PRACTICE   *Talk with another student about the pictures above. Use the past tense.*

Student 1: What did Carmen do first?
Student 2: She ....
Student 1: Then what did she do?
Student 2: She ....

PAIR PRACTICE   *Talk about the pictures above. Use the past tense.*

Student 1: Did Carmen .... before or after she ....?
Student 2: She .... before/after she ....

GRAMMAR   Non-separable Two-Word Verbs

• In non-separable two-word verbs, the verb and the particle stay together, and the object follows both parts.

EXAMPLES		Verb	Particle	Object
	Carmen	got	on	the bus.
	She	got	off	the bus.
	She	looked	for	some money.

READ   Make logical sentences with the words in the box.

	got		money.
I	didn't get	for	a bus.
	looked	on	a train.
Carmen	didn't look	off	her friends.
			an airplane.

READ

1. look for some money

2. get on the bus

3. get off the bus

4. get on the bus

5. get off the bus

6. look for a letter

PAIR PRACTICE   Talk to another student about the pictures above. Use the past tense.

Student 1: What did Carmen do at ....?
Student 2: She ....

GRAMMAR   Separable Two-Word Verbs

- In separable two-word verbs, the two parts (verb and particle) can be separated by an object, but when pronouns are used, they **must** go between the two parts.

EXAMPLES   *Object*

She	turned	off	the machine.	
She	turned		the machine	off.
She	turned		it	off.

It is **incorrect** to say, "She turned off it."

- Here are some common particles and their meanings:

Particles		Meanings
on	=	in operation, working, attached
off	=	not in operation, not working, unattached
up	=	completely, entirely, thoroughly
away	=	moving from you to a distance

EXAMPLES   *Particles*

Carmen	**put**	**on**	her work clothes.
She	**cleaned**	**up**	a mess.
She	**threw**	**away**	the broken pieces.
She	**took**	**out**	some change.
She	**took**	**off**	her coat.
She	**set**	**up**	her equipment.
She	**turned**	**on**	the machine.
She	**picked**	**up**	the tools.
She	**turned**	**off**	the machine.
She	**put**	**down**	the tools.

READ   Make logical complete sentences with the words in the boxes.

	put	away	the tools?			put		away.
	turn	down	the machine?			turned		down.
	take	up	her coat?			took	it	up.
Did Carmen	pick	on	money?		Yes, she	picked		on.
	clean	off	a mess?			cleaned	them	off.
	throw	out	the pieces?			threw		out.
	set		the equipment?			set		

PAIR PRACTICE

Talk with another student using the phrases below. Use nouns in the answers.
***Do not** separate the two-word verbs.*

Student 1: Please ....
Student 2: Do what?
Student 1: Please .... the ....

1. turn on the machine
2. turn off the machine
3. pick up the tools
4. put down the tools
5. put on the safety glasses

6. take off the glasses
7. clean up the mess
8. throw away the cups
9. set up the equipment
10. give back the money

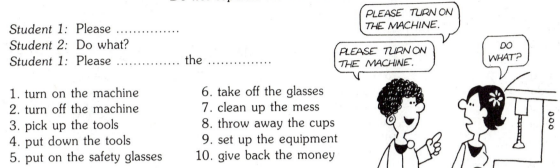

PAIR PRACTICE

Do the same exercise. This time separate the two parts of the two-word verbs.

Student 1: Please ....
Student 2: Do what?
Student 1: Please .... the ....

1. turn on the machine
2. turn off the machine
3. pick up the tools
4. put down the tools
5. put on the safety glasses

6. take off the glasses
7. clean up the mess
8. throw away the cups
9. set up the equipment
10. give back the money

PAIR PRACTICE

This time replace the noun with a pronoun. Notice that the two parts of the two-word verbs are separated.

Student 1: Please ....
Student 2: What do you want me to do?
Student 1: I want you to .... it/them ....

1. throw the broken pieces away
2. turn the T.V. on
3. turn the radio off
4. pick your clothes up
5. put that bottle down

6. put your sweater on
7. take that watch off
8. clean your room up
9. set the game up
10. give the money back

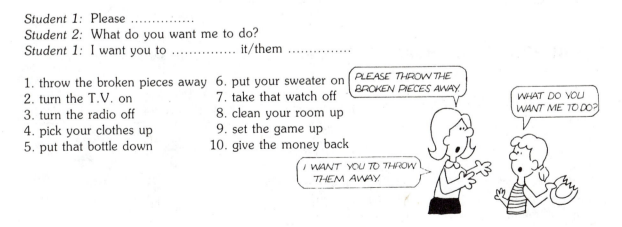

PAIR PRACTICE

Use the two-word verbs below and supply your own nouns. Use pronouns in the answers.

Student 1: Can I .... the ....?
Student 2: Sure, you can .... it/them ....

1. put on
2. put down
3. pick up
4. turn on
5. throw away

6. take off
7. take out
8. clean up
9. set up
10. give back

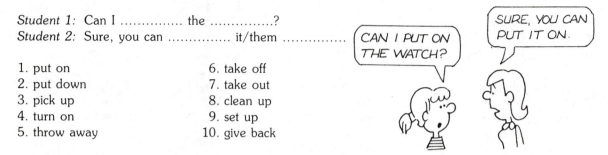

WRITE

Fill in the spaces below with the words in the box, and then match the questions with the answers.

up	away	down
on	for	back

1. When did you wake _up_ ?
2. What did you put _____?
3. What did you clean _____?
4. What did you throw _____?
5. What did you look _____?
6. What did you turn _____?
7. What did you get _____?
8. What did you set _____?
9. What did you pick _____?

a. A mess.
b. Some money.
c. At 8:30.
d. A machine.
e. The wrong bus.
f. The tools.
g. My work clothes.
h. The broken pieces.
i. My equipment.

PAIR PRACTICE

Use the present tense. Ask questions with the phrases below. Answer in your own words.

Student 1: When/Where do you usually ....?
Student 2: I usually ....

1. wake up
2. get up
3. put on your clothes
4. get on the bus
5. get off the bus
6. take off your shoes

7. turn on the T.V.
8. turn off the T.V.
9. throw away the garbage
10. look for money
11. go back home
12. set up your equipment

WRITE   *Fill in the spaces below with the words in the box. Then act out the commands in class.*

in	out	off	back	on	up	down	for	around	away

1. Take your watch *off*, and put it *down* on the table. Now, pick it *up*, give it to a student, and then take it *back*. Stand *up*, go to the waste basket, but don't throw your watch *away*. Put it *on* and go *back* to your seat.

2. Stand _____, go to the door, open it, look _____ the hall, but don't go _____. Close the door. Go to the light switch and turn it _____. Now, turn the light _____ again. Go _____ to your seat and sit _____.

3. Take _____ your wallet or purse. Open it and look _____ some money. Take a coin _____ and stand _____. Walk to the teacher's desk and give the coin to the teacher. Take it _____ and put it _____ your pocket. Turn _____ and go _____ to your seat.

4. Stand _____. Walk _____ the room and look _____ a pair of glasses. Pick _____ the glasses and put them _____. Take them _____ and give them _____. Walk _____ to your seat and sit _____.

CHALLENGE   *Write a series of commands and practice them in class. Use the examples above as models.*

_____

_____

_____

_____

_____

_____

_____

_____

_____

WRITE   *Fill in the spaces with the correct form of the past tense.*

Carmen's friend, George, is telling her about his day.

Carmen: And how was your day?

George: I (1) _**woke up**_ late today, too. My alarm clock (2) _____.
wake up   doesn't ring

I (3) _____, (4) _____ a shower, and
get up   take

(5) _____ my work clothes quickly. I (6) _____ to the kit-
put on   go

chen for some coffee, but there (7) _____ any. I
isn't

(8) _____ my car and (9) _____ the radio to listen to the
get in   turn on

morning news, but it (10) _____. Suddenly, my car
doesn't work

(11) _____; it (12) _____ any gas. I (13) _____
stops   doesn't have   get out

of the car and (14) _____ to push it. A few people
begin

(15) _____ me push it to a gas station. Then I (16) _____
help   realize

that I (17) _____ my wallet. The gas station attendant
don't have

(18) _____ very nice, and he (19) _____ me a little gas to
is   gives

get to work. Finally, when I (20) _____ at work, the parking lot
arrive

(21) _____ full, so I (22) _____ park on the street. And
is   have to

yes, you (23) _____ it. I (24) _____ a parking ticket!
guess   get

What a day!

PAIR PRACTICE

Fold the page down the middle. Look only at your side. Do the exercise orally.

Student 1	Student 2

Student 1

Listen to the questions from your partner and find the answers in the pictures below.

Now ask your partner these questions.

1. What can you go up?
2. Is it possible to go around the lake?
3. What can you go around?
4. Is it possible to go across the street?
5. What can you go up, go in, go down, go out, go across, and go around?

Student 2

Ask your partner these questions.

1. What items are pictured?
2. What items can you turn on?
3. What items can you put on?
4. Is it possible to pick up all the items?
5. What items can you get on?
6. What items can you put down, turn off, turn on, clean up, throw away, and take out?

Listen to your partner's questions. Find the answers in the picture below.

FOLD HERE

FOLD HERE

PRONUNCIATION   The /ər/ Sound

- *We pronounce many vowels before **r** like the /ər/ sound in the word **her**.*

- */ər/ represents the sound of any of the vowels followed by **r** when stressed.*

EXAMPLES

1. sh<u>ir</u>t   2. thi<u>r</u>sty   3. w<u>or</u>k   4. coll<u>ar</u>

5. Sat<u>ur</u>day   6. n<u>ur</u>se   7. moth<u>er</u>   8. numb<u>er</u>s

LISTEN   *Listen to the three words in each set below. Circle the word that has the /ər/ sound.*

1. (skirt)	read	haircut	6. Thursday	drive	more
2. hire	first	run	7. fruit	November	fire
3. car	truck	teacher	8. were	carry	write
4. wrong	doctor	dark	9. dark	street	dollar
5. third	rain	your	10. learn	program	rest

WRITE   *Fill in the spaces with the letters **or**, **ir**, **er**, or **ur**.*

1. I saw a pict_ur_e of h_er_ moth_er_ and fath_er_ at ch_ur_ch on Novemb_er_ th_ir_d.
2. The store cl____k showed the two g____ls some new summ____ sk____ts.
3. The n____se w____ked for the doct____ on Th____sdays and Sat____days for only a few doll____s.
4. The th____sty farm____ changed his d____ty sh____t before dinn____.

AT THE SUPERMARKET

COMPETENCIES	• Reading a Supermarket Directory
	• Understanding U.S. Measurements
	• Reading a Simple Recipe
	• Reading an Ad
	• Comparing Prices and Determining Savings
GRAMMAR	• *of*
VOCABULARY	• Common Shopping Terms
	• Food Containers and Measurements
	• Common Food Items
WORD BUILDING	• The Suffix *-ish*

LISTEN

The Barns family is doing the weekly shopping. Roy is pushing the shopping cart.

Roy: Do you have the shopping list?
Nancy: Yes, here it is. I brought the newspaper ad and the coupons, too.
Roy: Good. Do we need any sugar?
Nancy: Yes, we do. Get a bag.
Roy: Where's the sugar?
Nancy: I don't know. Let's ask the clerk over there.

Roy: Excuse me, sir, can you tell me where I can find the sugar?
Clerk: It's in Section Five.
Roy: Thanks.
Clerk: You're welcome.
Nancy: You get the sugar, and I'll meet you at the check-out counter.

Nancy and her family are waiting in line. A woman and the cashier are talking.

Woman: Here are some coupons.
Cashier: That's $64.72 minus $5.25 for the coupons.
Woman: How much is the total?
Cashier: It's $59.47.
Woman: Here's $60.00.
Cashier: And here's your receipt and your change. Have a nice day.
Woman: And you, too.

UNDERSTAND   *Circle True, False, or We don't know.*

1. It's the weekend.	True	False	We don't know.
2. Nancy uses a shopping list.	True	False	We don't know.
3. The Barns don't have any sugar at home.	True	False	We don't know.
4. Nancy paid $64.72.	True	False	We don't know.
5. The woman saved $5.25.	True	False	We don't know.
6. The woman got 54 cents in change.	True	False	We don't know.

READ

DIRECTORY			
Items	Section	Items	Section
Canned Fruit	2	Juices and Sodas	2
Canned Vegetables	3	Frozen Foods	11
Canned Fish and Meat	4	Cookies and Crackers	5
Baking (Flour, Oil)	5	Cereals	5
Sugar	5	Pet Food	6
Candy	6	Ice Cream	11
Detergents and Soap	12	Coffee and Tea	6
Paper Goods	6	Bakery	1
Shampoo and Toothpaste	9	Dairy Products	10
Waxes and Polish	12	Meat	8
Fresh Produce	14	Houseware Items	7
Frozen Vegetables	11	Liquor	13
Delicatessen	16	Plants and Flowers	15

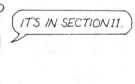

PAIR PRACTICE   *Talk with another student. Use the directory above.*

Student 1: Where is/are ....?
Student 2: It is/They are ....

PAIR PRACTICE   *Use the directory above.*

Student 1: What's in Section ....?
Student 2: .... is/are in Section ....

CHALLENGE   *Alphabetize the directory above.*

WRITE   *Match the questions with the pictures. Write the letters of the pictures in the blanks after the questions.*

1. Where are the canned vegetables? _d_

2. Where's the detergent? _____

3. Where's the produce? _____

4. Where are the frozen vegetables? _____

5. Where's the bakery? _____

6. Where are the dairy products? _____

7. Where are the houseware items? _____

8. Where are the paper goods? _____

a. FROZEN CORN   b. SOAP POWDER

c.   d. PEAS CORN

e. RYE   f. MILK BUTTER

g.   h.

WRITE   *Match the pictures with the sentences. Write the letters of the pictures in the blanks after the sentences.*

Where is/are the ....?

a. TUNA   b.

c. FROZEN BEANS   d.

e. DOG YUMS   f.

g.   h. WINE

1. The paper goods are in Section 6. _b_

2. The pet food is in Section 6. _____

3. Fresh produce is in Section 14. _____

4. Meat is in Section 8. _____

5. Canned fish is in Section 4. _____

6. Frozen food is in Section 11. _____

7. Cookies are in Section 5. _____

8. Liquor is in Section 13. _____

READ   *Food Containers*

Roy's putting the food on the counter.

PAIR PRACTICE   *Talk with another student about the picture above.*

Student 1: What's on the counter?
Student 2: There's a .... of ....

PAIR PRACTICE   *Use the picture above.*

Student 1: What's in the ....?
Student 2: Some ....

PAIR PRACTICE   *Use the picture above.*

Student 1: What kind of container does/containers do .... come in?
Student 2: It comes/They come in a ....

GRAMMAR *of*

- *We use the preposition **of** to show that one thing contains something else.*

EXAMPLES

a six-pack	**of**	soda
a carton	**of**	milk
a sack	**of**	flour
a bottle	**of**	cooking oil

READ *Make logical complete sentences with the words in the box.*

Please get me a	tube carton sack bottle jar bag box six-pack can package	of	napkins. soda. potatoes. ice cream. toothpaste. wine. jam. potato chips. cereal.

PAIR PRACTICE *Talk with another student. Use the pictures below.*

Student 1: How many .... of .... are there?
Student 2: There is/are .... of ....

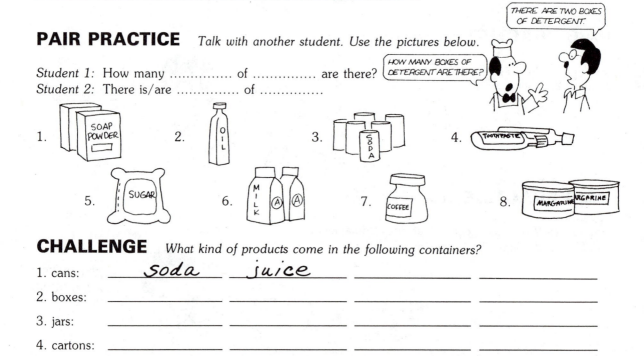

CHALLENGE *What kind of products come in the following containers?*

1. cans: ____soda____ ____juice____ _____ _____
2. boxes: _____ _____ _____ _____
3. jars: _____ _____ _____ _____
4. cartons: _____ _____ _____ _____
5. bottles: _____ _____ _____ _____

READ   *Measurement*

Roy and the kids are putting some more food on the counter.

PAIR PRACTICE   *Talk with another student about the picture above.*

Student 1: What's on the counter?
Student 2: There is/are .... of ....

PAIR PRACTICE   *Use the picture above.*

Student 1: How much/many ....?
Student 2: There is/are ....

CHALLENGE   *What comes in the following measurements?*

1. slices: *cheese*   *bread*   _____   _____

2. rolls: _____   _____   _____   _____

3. pieces: _____   _____   _____   _____

READ *Liquid Measurement*

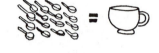

3 teaspoons (tsp.) =
1 tablespoon (Tb.)

16 tablespoons = 1 cup

2 cups = 1 pint (pt.)

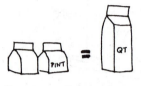

2 pints = 1 quart*

4 quarts (qt.) = 1 gallon (gal.)

READ *Weight*

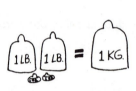

16 ounces (oz.) =
1 pound (lb.)

2.2 pounds (lbs.) =
1 kilogram

SPOONS AND CUPS	LIQUID OUNCES	LIQUID GRAMS
1 tsp. (teaspoon)	1/6	5
1 Tb. (tablespoon)	1/2	15
1 cup (16 Tb.)	8	227
2 cups (1 pint)	16 (1 pound)	454
4 cups (1 quart)	32	907
6 2/3 Tb.	3 1/2	100
1 cup plus 1 Tb.	8 1/2	250
4 1/3 cups	2.2 pounds	1000 (1 kilogram)

PAIR PRACTICE *Talk with another student. Use the information above.*

Student 1: How many .... are there in a ....?
Student 2: There are .... in a ....

THERE ARE 16 OUNCES IN A POUND.

HOW MANY OUNCES ARE THERE IN A POUND?

CHALLENGE *In what liquid measurement or weight can you find the items below?*

1. sugar   *pounds*
2. milk   _____
3. cream   _____
4. potatoes   _____
5. juice   _____

6. flour   _____
7. butter   _____
8. apples   _____
9. coffee   _____
10. cereal   _____

CHALLENGE *How many pounds do you weigh? I weigh _____ pounds.*

---

* A quart is almost equal to a liter.

READ

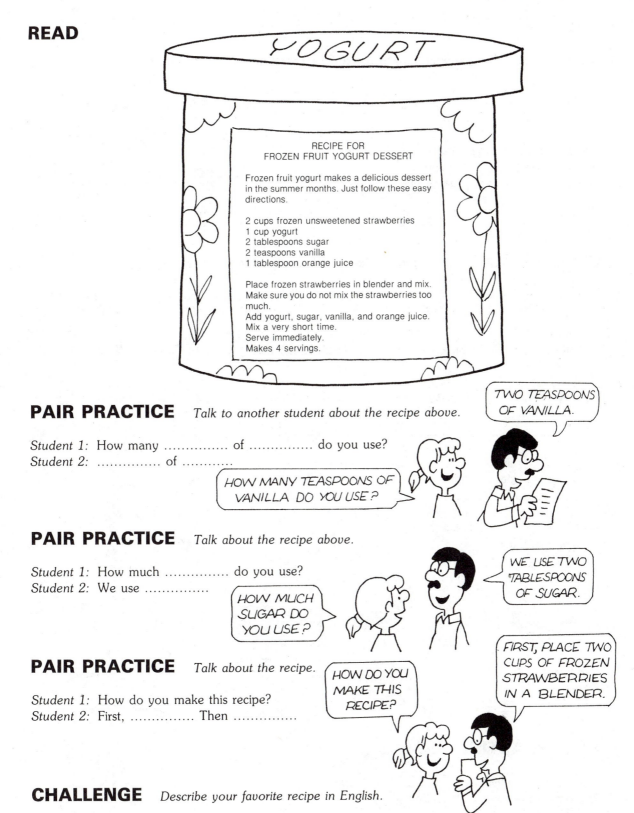

YOGURT

RECIPE FOR
FROZEN FRUIT YOGURT DESSERT

Frozen fruit yogurt makes a delicious dessert
in the summer months. Just follow these easy
directions.

2 cups frozen unsweetened strawberries
1 cup yogurt
2 tablespoons sugar
2 teaspoons vanilla
1 tablespoon orange juice

Place frozen strawberries in blender and mix.
Make sure you do not mix the strawberries too
much.
Add yogurt, sugar, vanilla, and orange juice.
Mix a very short time.
Serve immediately.
Makes 4 servings.

PAIR PRACTICE   *Talk to another student about the recipe above.*

Student 1: How many .... of .... do you use?
Student 2: .... of ....

TWO TEASPOONS OF VANILLA.

HOW MANY TEASPOONS OF VANILLA DO YOU USE?

PAIR PRACTICE   *Talk about the recipe above.*

Student 1: How much .... do you use?
Student 2: We use ....

WE USE TWO TABLESPOONS OF SUGAR.

HOW MUCH SUGAR DO YOU USE?

PAIR PRACTICE   *Talk about the recipe.*

Student 1: How do you make this recipe?
Student 2: First, ... Then ....

HOW DO YOU MAKE THIS RECIPE?

FIRST, PLACE TWO CUPS OF FROZEN STRAWBERRIES IN A BLENDER.

CHALLENGE   *Describe your favorite recipe in English.*

READ

Nancy wants to buy some salami in the delicatessen section of the store.

Nancy: Please give me some salami. How do you sell it?
Clerk: We sell it by the pound.
Nancy: OK. Give me a quarter pound of salami.
Clerk: Will that be all?
Nancy: No, give me a half-pound of potato salad, too.

UNDERSTAND   *Circle **True**, **False**, or **We don't know**.*

1. Nancy wants to buy a few slices of salami.	True	False	We don't know.
2. Nancy wants to buy 4 oz. of salami.	True	False	We don't know.
3. Nancy wants to buy 100 grams of potato salad.	True	False	We don't know.
4. The salami and the potato salad together weigh 12 ounces.	True	False	We don't know.

PAIR PRACTICE   *Talk with another student about the foods below. Use the preposition **by** with the words in the box.*

bunch	head	pound	slice	ounce
quart	loaf	pint	piece	roll

Student 1: How do you sell ....?
Student 2: By the ....

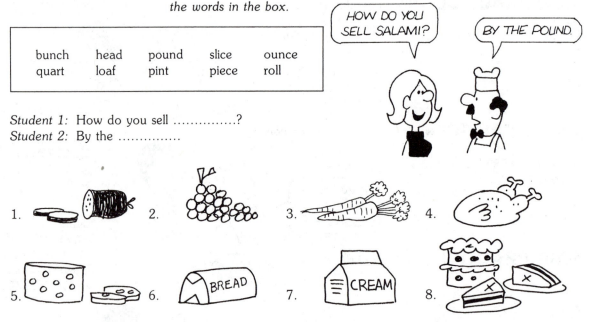

PAIR PRACTICE   *Use the vocabulary and pictures from the exercise above.*

Student 1: Is it possible to buy .... by the ....?
Student 2: Yes, it is. / No, it isn't.

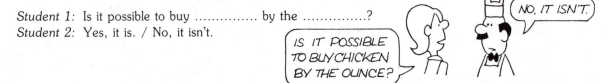

READ

SHOPPING LIST

1 bottle of cooking oil
1 jar of coffee
2 bunches of bananas
2 heads of lettuce
3 loaves of bread
1 pound of hamburger
3 quarts of milk
1 roll of paper towels
2 bars of soap
1 bag of sugar
1 box of detergent
1 sack of flour
3 cans of orange juice
2 packages of cookies
2 tubes of toothpaste
2 tubs of margarine

DIRECTORY

ITEMS	SECTION
Dairy Products	10
Baking	5
Coffee and Tea	6
Juices and Soda	2
Detergent and Soap	12
Shampoo and Toothpaste	9
Sugar	5
Paper Goods	6
Cookies and Crackers	5
Meat	8
Bakery	1
Fresh Produce	14

PAIR PRACTICE   *Talk with another student about the two lists above.*

Student 1: Where can I find ....?
Student 2: It's/They're in Section ....
Student 1: How many .... do you want?
Student 2: Give me .... of ....

WHERE CAN I FIND SOME SOAP?

HOW MANY BARS DO YOU WANT?

IT'S IN SECTION 12.

GIVE ME TWO BARS OF SOAP.

CHALLENGE   *Alphabetize the directory above.*

READ

A AND B MARKET

ITEM	SIZE	PRICE
SHAMPOO	8 oz. bottle	$1.99
DETERGENT	49 oz. box	2.25
PAPER NAPKINS	360 in pkg.	1.49
DEODORANT	2 1/2 oz. bottle	2.99
COFFEE	1 lb. can	4.71
FROZEN ORANGE JUICE	12 oz. can	.89
LARGE EGGS	1 dozen ctn.	.79
CABBAGE	3 heads	1.00
SLICED CHEESE	5 oz. pkg.	.99
SAUSAGE	8 oz. pkg.	2.53
APPLES	3 lbs. bag	.98
GROUND BEEF	1 lb. pkg.	1.79
CHICKEN	1 lb.	.69

COUPON
SOUP
15¢ off
8 oz. can
expires Jan. 1

COUPON
MARGARINE
Save 29 ¢
1 lb. pkg.

Abbreviations:
lb. — pound
oz. — ounce
ctn. — carton
pkg. — package

PAIR PRACTICE   *Talk with another student about the ad above.*

Student 1: How much do/does .... cost?
Student 2: .... cost/costs $...............

HOW MUCH DO TWO BOTTLES OF SHAMPOO COST?

TWO BOTTLES OF SHAMPOO COST $3.98.

WRITE   *Complete the dialog with your own words.*

Nancy: *Can you tell me where the milk is?*

Clerk: _____

Nancy: I looked there. I saw only small cartons of milk. I want a large size.

Clerk: Did you look near the eggs?

Nancy: _____

Clerk: Wait here. I'll get you a large carton of milk. What size do you want?

Nancy: _____

Clerk: Here you are. Is this half gallon size OK?

Nancy: _____

Clerk: _____

Nancy: _____

CHALLENGE   *Write a short dialog. You are at the supermarket, and you want to know the price of a product and where to find it in the market.*

You: *Excuse me.* _____

Clerk: _____

You: _____

Clerk: _____

You: _____

Clerk: _____

You: _____

Clerk: _____

CHALLENGE   *Practice your dialog with another student, and then present it in front of the class.*

DICTATION   *Cover the sentences under each line. Write the dictation on the line as your teacher reads it to you. Then uncover the sentences and correct your writing.*

Dear Roy,

1. _____

   I'll be home a little late tonight.

2. _____

   Please go to the supermarket and get a few things for dinner.

3. _____

   Get a quart of milk, a loaf of bread, and a jar of coffee.

4. _____

   Here's twenty dollars for the food.

5. _____

   Don't buy any ice cream. Remember your diet!

6. _____

   See you about 6:30.

   Love, Nancy

WRITE   *Write a note to a person in your home. Tell him or her to go to the supermarket and buy some food.*

Dear _____ ,

I can't do the shopping today. Please go _____

_____

_____

_____

_____

_____

Here's $ _____

See you at _____ *p.m.*

PAIR PRACTICE

Fold the page down the middle. Look only at your side. Do the exercise orally.

Student 1

Listen to the questions from your partner and find the answers in the signs below.

Abbreviations
reg. = regular price
lb. = pound

Now ask your partner these questions.

1. Is bread on sale?
2. How many oranges can you buy for $1.50?
3. How much does tomato juice cost without a coupon?
4. How much do five bars of soap cost?
5. How much does a loaf of bread cost?
6. Is soap on sale?

Student 2

Ask your partner these questions.

1. How much do two bottles of wine cost?
2. How many rolls of paper towels can you buy for 98 cents?
3. How much does one package of frozen vegetables cost?
4. How much do four pounds of apples cost?
5. Can you buy three bottles of wine for $6.00?
6. How much did frozen vegetables cost yesterday?
7. Can you buy four bottles of wine for $10.00?

Listen to the questions from your partner and find the answers in the signs below.

Abbreviations
per = each item
ea. = each item
reg. = regular price

WORD BUILDING   *The Suffix -ish*

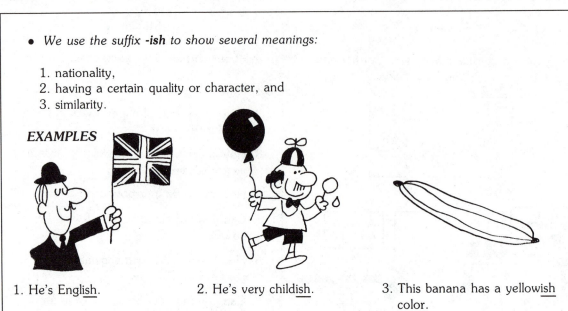

- *We use the suffix **-ish** to show several meanings:*

  1. nationality,
  2. having a certain quality or character, and
  3. similarity.

EXAMPLES

1. He's English.

2. He's very childish.

3. This banana has a yellowish color.

WRITE   *Describe the colors of the following fruits and vegetables.*

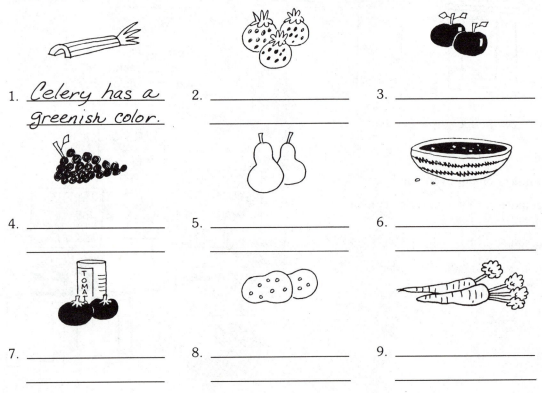

1. *Celery has a greenish color.*

2. _____

3. _____

4. _____

5. _____

6. _____

7. _____

8. _____

9. _____

WHERE DOES IT HURT?

COMPETENCIES	• Making a Medical Appointment • Describing Medical Problems • Filling Out Medical Forms
GRAMMAR	• *would like* • *that* with Clauses • More Irregular Verbs • *say* and *tell*
VOCABULARY	• General Medical Terms • Parts of the Body • Symptoms and Illnesses
SPELLING	• The Silent *gh*

LISTEN

Betty Fuller is calling her doctor to make an appointment.

A few minutes later.

Receptionist: Thank you for waiting. Now may I help you?
     Betty: Yes, I would like to make an appointment with Dr. Snow.
Receptionist: What's the problem?
     Betty: I'd like to have a general physical examination and I'd like him to look at my left hand. It hurts a little when I open and close it.
Receptionist: Dr. Snow is booked up all this week. Can you come in next Tuesday at 10:00 a.m.?
     Betty: That's fine.
Receptionist: Would you like me to call you if there is a cancellation?
     Betty: Yes, please do.

UNDERSTAND *Circle True, False, or We don't know.*

1. Betty doesn't feel very well.	True	False	We don't know.
2. "Can you hold?" means "Can you wait?"	True	False	We don't know.
3. "Booked up" means "The doctor is reading."	True	False	We don't know.
4. Betty's appointment is next Tuesday.	True	False	We don't know.
5. Dr. Snow is a woman.	True	False	We don't know.
6. The receptionist will call Betty if a patient can not keep an appointment.	True	False	We don't know.

GRAMMAR   *would like*

- *The expression **would like** means **want**, but it is more polite.*
- *The contraction of **would like** is **'d like**.*

EXAMPLES

Affirmative

I	**would**	**like**	to make an appointment.
You	**'d**	**like**	to have a physical examination.
She	**'d**	**like**	the doctor to see her left hand.

Negative

| I | **wouldn't** | **like** | to have a late appointment. |

Question

| **Would** | you | **like** | me to call you? |

READ   *Make logical complete sentences with the words in the box.*

| I He She They | would 'd wouldn't | like | to make an appointment. to see the doctor. to cancel my appointment. to have a physical examination. to speak to the doctor. you to call me. the doctor to look at my hand. |

PAIR PRACTICE   *Talk with another student. Use the phrases below.*

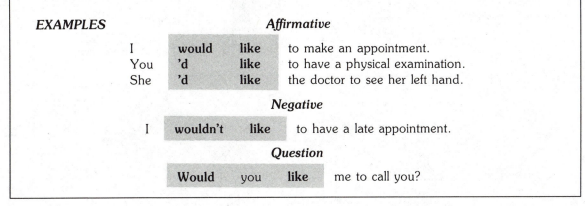

Student 1: What would you like?
Student 2: I'd like to make an appointment with ....
              or
          I'd like to see the ....
              or
          I'd like to speak with ....

WHAT WOULD YOU LIKE?

I'D LIKE TO MAKE AN APPOINTMENT WITH A DOCTOR.

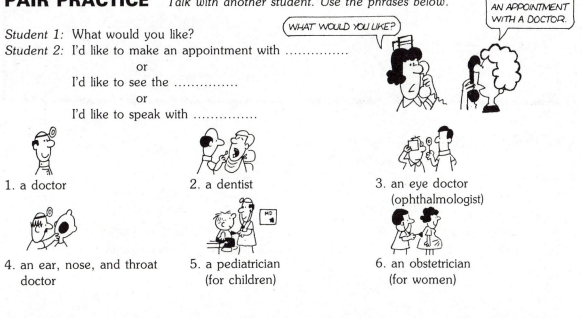

1. a doctor

2. a dentist

3. an eye doctor (ophthalmologist)

4. an ear, nose, and throat doctor

5. a pediatrician (for children)

6. an obstetrician (for women)

READ

Betty's at the hospital.

MAY I HELP YOU?

IT'LL BE A FEW MINUTES. PLEASE SIT DOWN AND FILL OUT THIS FORM.

YES, I HAVE A 10 O'CLOCK APPOINTMENT WITH DR. SNOW.

PLEASE PRINT

Name: *Fuller*   *Betty*   *Louise*
            Last   First   Middle

Address: *6534   Hillside St. Los Angeles 90030* Telephone: *555-1024*
         Number   Street   City   Zip

Date of Birth: *April 7, 1934*   Place of Birth: *Columbus, Ohio*
              Month/Date/Year

1. Do you have any medical insurance? (check one) Yes *✓*   No _____
2. Name of medical insurance company: *Bluecare Ins.* Policy number # *6941003*
3. What's the reason for this visit? *Physical examination*
4. Are you taking any medicine now? (check one) Yes _____   No *✓*

   If so, what kind of medicine? *—*

5. Are you allergic to any medicine? (check one) Yes *✓*   No _____

   If so, what kind of medicine? *penicillin*

6. Are you having any pain at this time? (check one) Yes *✓*   No _____
7. Are you in good health? (check one) Yes *✓*   No _____
8. Do you smoke, drink, or take drugs? (check one) Yes _____   No *✓*

Today's date: *May 4th*   Signature: *Betty Fuller*

UNDERSTAND   *Circle **True**, **False**, or **We don't know**.*

1. Betty has medical insurance.	True	False	We don't know.
2. Betty is 50 years old.	True	False	We don't know.
3. "If so" means "If the answer is yes."	True	False	We don't know.
4. Betty is allergic to penicillin.	True	False	We don't know.
5. Betty smokes.	True	False	We don't know.

READ *Use your dictionary.*

The nurse forgot to give Betty a second form.

EXCUSE ME, MA'AM, BUT I HAVE TO GIVE YOU ANOTHER FORM. PLEASE FILL IT OUT, TOO.

HEALTH EXAMINATION RECORD

NAME: *Betty Fuller*   DATE: *May 4, 1984*

ADDRESS: *6534 Hillside St., L.A.*   PHONE: *555-1024*

AGE: *50*   SEX: (circle one)   Male   (Female)   BIRTHDATE: *4/7/34*

MEDICAL HISTORY

Did you ever have one of the following? (check ✔)

ILLNESSES	DISEASES	SURGERIES	DATE
Frequent fevers _____	Measles ✔	1. *Leg*	*1956*
Frequent colds _____	Mumps _____	2. _____	_____
Frequent headaches _____	Chicken Pox ✔	3. _____	_____
Frequent sore throats _____	Polio _____		
Frequent upset stomach _____	Scarlet Fever _____	MEDICATION YOU	
Allergies *✔ cats and dust*	Whooping Cough _____	ARE SENSITIVE TO	
Serious injuries _____	Other _____		
Kidney trouble _____			
Tuberculosis _____	IMMUNIZATIONS/TESTS	1. *penicillin*	
Convulsions _____		2. _____	
Diabetes _____	Polio ✔	3. _____	
Blood diseases _____	Diphtheria _____		
High blood pressure _____	Whooping Cough _____	MEDICATION YOU	
Heart trouble _____	Tetanus ✔	ARE TAKING NOW	
Mental problems _____	Smallpox ✔		
Liver trouble _____	Typhoid _____	1. *none*	
Nervousness _____	Tuberculin ✔	2. _____	
Arthritis _____	Other _____	3. _____	

PAIR PRACTICE *Talk with another student about Betty's health record.*

Student 1: Did Betty ever have ....?
Student 2: Yes, she did. / No, she didn't.

DID BETTY EVER HAVE AN OPERATION?

YES, SHE DID.

Wanda Bratko's also in the waiting room. She's asking Betty for help.

> EXCUSE ME. I HAVE TO FILL OUT THIS FORM. I DON'T UNDERSTAND ALL THE MEDICAL WORDS. CAN YOU EXPLAIN THEM TO ME?

> I'LL TRY.

WRITE   *Match the questions and answers. Write the letters of the answers in the blanks after the questions.*

1. What's a fever? _____ f _____

2. What's an allergy? _____

3. What's an upset stomach? _____

4. What's diabetes? _____

5. What's heart trouble? _____

6. What is a headache? _____

7. What is an injury? _____

8. What's a sore throat? _____

9. What's arthritis? _____

a.   It's being unable to move your joints.

b.   It's being unable to keep food in your stomach.

c.   It's a bad reaction to plants, animals, medicine, or food.

d.   It's the inability of your body to use sugar.

e.   It's pain in your head.

f.   It's a high body temperature.

g.   It's having a weak heart.

h.   It's a wound or other damage to the body.

i.   It's pain in your throat.

PAIR PRACTICE   *Talk with another student. Use the cues below.*

Student 1: What's the matter with that ....?
Student 2: He/She has ....

> WHAT'S THE MATTER WITH THAT MAN?

> HE HAS A HEADACHE.

1. a headache   2. a sore throat   3. a rash   4. a toothache

5. a broken leg   6. a stomach ache   7. the chills   8. a fever

WRITE   *Fill out the form below.*

PLEASE PRINT

Name: _____
  Last   First   Middle

Address: _____ Telephone: _____
  Number Street   City

Date of Birth: _____ Place of Birth: _____
  Month/Date/Year

1. Do you have any medical insurance? (check one) Yes _____ No _____
2. Name of medical insurance company: _____ Policy number #_____
3. What's the reason for this visit? _____
4. Are you taking any medicine now? (check one) Yes _____ No _____
    If so, what kind of medicine? _____
5. Are you allergic to any medicine? (check one) Yes _____ No _____
    If so, what kind of medicine? _____
6. Are you having any pain at this time? (check one) Yes _____ No _____
7. Are you in good health? (check one) Yes _____ No _____
8. Do you smoke, drink, or take drugs? (check one) Yes _____ No _____

AGE: _____   SEX: (circle one) Male   Female

MEDICAL HISTORY

Did you ever have one of the following? (check ✔)

ILLNESSES   DISEASES   SURGERIES   DATE

Frequent fevers _____ Measles _____ 1. _____ _____
Frequent colds _____ Mumps _____   2. _____ _____
Frequent headaches ____ Chicken Pox _____ 3. _____ _____
Frequent sore throats __ Polio _____
Frequent upset stomach_ Scarlet Fever _____ MEDICATION YOU
Allergies _____   Whooping Cough _____ ARE SENSITIVE TO
Serious injuries _____ Other _____
Kidney trouble _____
Tuberculosis _____ IMMUNIZATIONS/TESTS   1. _____
Convulsions _____   2. _____
Diabetes _____   Polio _____   3. _____
Blood diseases _____ Diphtheria _____
High blood pressure ___ Whooping Cough _____ MEDICATION YOU
Heart trouble _____ Tetanus _____   ARE TAKING NOW
Mental problems _____   Smallpox _____
Liver trouble _____ Typhoid _____   1. _____
Nervousness _____   Tuberculin _____   2. _____
Arthritis _____   Other _____   3. _____

DATE: _____   SIGNATURE: _____

LISTEN

Betty is speaking to the doctor.

Doctor: What's the matter?
  Betty: My left hand hurts. I have a pain in my wrist.
Doctor: When did you first notice the problem?
  Betty: A few weeks ago.
Doctor: Let me examine it.

(A few minutes later.)

Doctor: It's probably arthritis. I can write you a prescription for some cream. Do you
        have any other problems?
  Betty: No, I don't. I made this appointment for a general physical examination.
Doctor: When was your last exam?
  Betty: Five years ago.
Doctor: I'll examine you here. Then take these papers to the laboratory for an X-ray,
        and urine and blood tests. When I get the test results, I'll call you.

UNDERSTAND   *Circle True, False, or We don't know.*

1. Betty's right hand hurts.	True	False	We don't know.
2. Betty's problem began last month.	True	False	We don't know.
3. Betty has arthritis.	True	False	We don't know.
4. Arthritis is a disease.	True	False	We don't know.
5. Only doctors can write prescriptions.	True	False	We don't know.
6. The doctor will have the test results next week.	True	False	We don't know.

READ   *Study the parts of the body.*

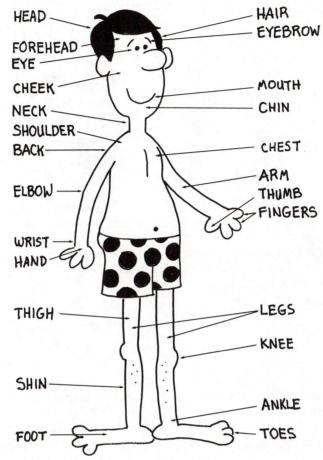

HEAD — HAIR
EYEBROW
FOREHEAD —
EYE —
CHEEK —
NECK —
SHOULDER —
BACK —
ELBOW —
WRIST —
HAND —
THIGH —
SHIN —
FOOT —

— HAIR
— EYEBROW
— MOUTH
— CHIN
— CHEST
— ARM
— THUMB
— FINGERS
— LEGS
— KNEE
— ANKLE
— TOES

PAIR PRACTICE   *Talk with another student. Use the picture above.*

Student 1: Where does it hurt?
Student 2: My .... hurts.

WHERE DOES IT HURT?

MY LEFT HAND HURTS.

PAIR PRACTICE   *Use the picture above.*

Student 1: What's the matter?
Student 2: I have a pain in my ....

WHAT'S THE MATTER?

I HAVE A PAIN IN MY LEFT HAND.

READ

Betty meets Wanda in the elevator.

DIRECTORY

	Room
Emergency Room	101
Laboratory	102
X-ray Lab	103
Surgery	Basement
Intensive Care	201
Maternity	210
Dietary Service	110
Pharmacy	112
Wards	3rd–5th Floors

Betty: Oh, hello again.
Wanda: Hi. Can you tell me where the lab is?
Betty: No, I can't. Let's look at the directory over there.
Wanda: What do they do in the lab?
Betty: They take tests.

CHALLENGE   *Alphabetize the directory above.*

WRITE   *Match the questions and answers. Write the letters of the answers in the blanks after the questions.*

1. What do they do in the emergency room?
   ___e___

2. What happens in the X-ray lab? _____

3. What do they do in the intensive care unit?
   _____

4. What do they do in surgery? _____

5. What happens in maternity? _____

6. What do they do in dietary services?
   _____

7. What happens in the wards? _____

8. What do they do in the pharmacy?
   _____

a. They cook the patients' meals there.

b. Nurses take care of very sick patients.

c. They prepare medicine there.

d. Babies are born there.

e. A medical team gives quick help to victims of serious accidents or sudden illnesses.

f. They take pictures of the inside of your body.

g. The patients stay there.

h. Surgeons operate on patients there.

READ

It's the next day. Betty is telling Nancy about her visit to the doctor's.

Nancy: I heard that you went to the doctor's office yesterday.
Betty: That's right.
Nancy: Did you feel ill?
Betty: No, I felt fine except for a little arthritis in my left hand. I knew that it wasn't serious. I just thought that it was time for a general physical examination. The doctor understood my concern.
Nancy: Well, what did the doctor say?
Betty: He said that my arthritis wasn't bad. He told me that I was OK.
Nancy: Did he give you any medicine for your arthritis?
Betty: Yes, he wrote a prescription for some cream. He told me that I have to use it twice a day.
Nancy: Are you using it?
Betty: I forgot to use it last night, but I remembered this morning.
Nancy: Good. I'm glad that you're in good health.
Betty: So am I!

UNDERSTAND   *Circle True, False, or We don't know.*

1. Nancy's husband told her that Betty was at the hospital.	True	False	We don't know.
2. Betty has to take the medicine.	True	False	We don't know.
3. Betty uses the medicine in the morning and at night.	True	False	We don't know.
4. Betty is happy that she is in good health.	True	False	We don't know.

WRITE   *Underline the word **that** in the sentences above.*

GRAMMAR   *that* with Clauses

- *Many clauses begin with **that** and often follow verbs such as the following:*

Present	Past		Present	Past
hear	heard		tell	told
say	said		write	wrote
feel	felt		forget	forgot
know	knew		understand	understood
think	thought		remember	remembered

EXAMPLES

I		heard	**that**	you went to the doctor's office.
I		knew	**that**	it wasn't serious.
I		thought	**that**	it was time for a physical examination.
The doctor	told me		**that**	I was OK.
He		said	**that**	I had to use the medicine twice a day.

- *The word **that** is often deleted.*

EXAMPLES

I heard ~~that~~ you went to the doctor.
I knew ~~that~~ it wasn't serious.

READ   *Make logical complete sentences with the words in the box.*

I The doctor Betty Nancy	understood remembered heard knew thought said told forgot	that	you she Betty it I arthritis	visited the doctor. are taking medicine. wrote a prescription. wasn't serious. was in good health. had to use the medicine. was OK.

PAIR PRACTICE   *Talk with another student. Use the phrases below.*

Student 1: What do you know about ....?
Student 2: I think that it is/isn't serious.
        or
    I think that they are/aren't serious.

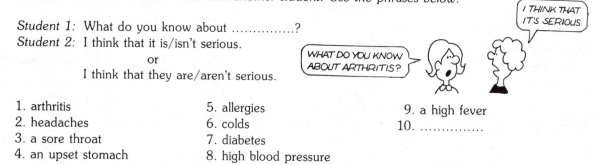

1. arthritis
2. headaches
3. a sore throat
4. an upset stomach
5. allergies
6. colds
7. diabetes
8. high blood pressure
9. a high fever
10. ....

WRITE   *Fill in the spaces below with the words in the box.*

Betty and Nancy are talking.

did	didn't	know	knew	forget	forgot	think	thought

Nancy: I didn't __know__ that you had arthritis.

Betty: Oh. I thought that you __knew__.

Nancy: I _____ that you had a sore hand, but I _____ _____ that

it was arthritis. _____ you _____ that I have a little arthritis, too?

Betty: No, I _____.

Nancy: _____ you _____ to use your medicine?

Betty: Yes, I _____. I _____ about it.

Nancy: Why _____ you _____?

Betty: I _____ because I don't usually use medicine.

Nancy: _____ you _____ your medicine this morning?

Betty: No, I _____ _____ to use the medicine today.

Nancy: _____ you _____ that you were ill?

Betty: No, I _____ _____ that I was sick. I just _____ that it was

time to have a physical examination.

Nancy: _____ you _____ that it was a good examination?

Betty: Yes, I _____. I _____ the doctor did a good job.

WRITE   *Fill in the spaces below with the words in the box.*

| did | didn't | understand | understood | hear | heard | feel | felt |

Nancy: *Did* you *understand* the doctor's directions?

Betty: Of course, I __*did*__. I _____ everything.

Nancy: _____ you _____ the medical forms?

Betty: Yes, I _____, but a woman in the waiting room _____

_____ all the items, so I helped her.

Betty: When _____ you _____ I went to the hospital?

Nancy: I _____ it this morning.

Betty: How _____ you _____ about it?

Nancy: I _____ it from Roy.

Betty: How _____ he _____ it?

Nancy: I don't know, but I think that he _____ it from your husband.

Betty: _____ you _____ that I was OK?

Nancy: No, I _____ _____ that. I only _____ that you were at the

hospital.

Nancy: How _____ you _____ yesterday?

Betty: I _____ fine.

Nancy: _____ your hand _____ OK, too?

Betty: No, it _____. It _____ a little sore.

Nancy: How _____ you _____ when you got your bill?

Betty: I _____ terrible.

READ

The next day there was a message on Betty's telephone answering machine.

> THIS IS DR. SNOW AT THE WESTEND HOSPITAL. I HAVE THE RESULTS OF YOUR TESTS. THEY SHOW THAT YOU DON'T HAVE ANY SERIOUS MEDICAL PROBLEMS. I'M HAPPY TO TELL YOU THAT YOU ARE IN VERY GOOD HEALTH.
>
> I HOPE THAT YOUR HAND IS BETTER. I BELIEVE THAT IT'S A MILD CASE OF ARTHRITIS; I DON'T THINK THAT IT'S SERIOUS. USE THE MEDICINE AND CALL WHEN YOU NEED MORE.

WRITE   *What did you find out from the telephone message? Complete the sentences with **that** and clauses.*

1. The doctor said *that he got the results of the test* .

2. The tests showed _____.

3. The doctor told Betty _____.

4. The doctor hoped _____.

5. The doctor believes _____.

6. The doctor doesn't think _____.

7. We know _____.

GRAMMAR   *say* and *tell*

- *The verbs **say** and **tell** have the same meaning, but they are used in different ways.*
- *They have irregular forms in the past tense: **said** and **told**.*
- *We use **tell** when we **tell somebody something**.*
- *We use **say** when we **say something (to somebody)**.*
- *We also use **tell** in expressions such as **tell a story, a lie,** or **a joke**.*

EXAMPLES		Somebody	Something
Betty	**said**		that her left hand hurt.
The doctor	**said**		that it wasn't serious.
Wanda	**said**		that she didn't understand the words.
The doctor	**said,**		"Go to the lab."
Betty	**told**	the doctor	that her left hand hurt.
The doctor	**told**	Betty	that it wasn't serious.
Wanda	**told**	Betty	that she didn't understand the words.
The doctor	**told**	her,	"Go to the lab."

READ   *Make logical complete sentences with the words in the box.*

I	said		about her visit to the doctor.
You	didn't say		that it wasn't serious.
He			that I didn't understand.
She	told	you	that I felt very well.
It	didn't tell	him	"Go to the laboratory."
We		her	"Call for more medicine."
They		them	"May I help you?"

PAIR PRACTICE   *Talk with another student. Use the cues below.*

Student 1: What did .... say/tell you?
Student 2: He/She said/told me, "..............."

1. (HELLO.)
2. (PLEASE HOLD.)
3. (PLEASE FILL OUT THIS FORM.)
4. (THE ARTHRITIS ISN'T SERIOUS.)
5. (PLEASE GO TO THE LAB.)
6. (THE TEST RESULTS WERE GOOD.)
7. (BETTY'S IN GOOD HEALTH)
8. (GOOD-BYE.)

(WHAT DID HE SAY?) (HE SAID HELLO.)

WRITE   *Fill in the spaces below with* **say**, **said**, **tell**, *or* **told**.

It is a week later. Betty is calling Nancy.

Betty: I heard that you went to the doctor, too. How are you?

Nancy: So-so.

Betty: What's the matter?

Nancy: I think that I have a cold.

Betty: Did you see a doctor?

Nancy: Yes, I did.

Betty: Well, what did he _**say**_?

Nancy: He _**said**_, "Take two aspirins."

Betty: What did you _____ the doctor?

Nancy: I _____ him that I had a sore throat. He _____ me, "Drink a

lot of liquids."

Betty: What else did he _____ you?

Nancy: He _____, "Gargle with a pinch of salt and warm water." I _____

the doctor that I felt terrible. He _____ that it wasn't serious. He

_____ that it was only a cold. He _____ me to go to bed and rest.

Betty: Is that all he _____ you?

Nancy: No, he _____ me that my bill was $50.00!

READ   *Reread the dialog above, but delete the word* **that** *from the clauses.*

SPELLING   The Silent *gh*

- *The letter combination **gh** is often silent.*

- *It is usually silent after the long **i** and **ô** sounds.*

- *It often appears in the past tense of irregular verbs.*

EXAMPLES

1. li<u>gh</u>t

2. ni<u>gh</u>t

3. ri<u>gh</u>t

4. The teacher tau<u>gh</u>t the class yesterday

5. The catcher cau<u>gh</u>t the ball.

6. The fighters fou<u>gh</u>t hard.

WRITE   *Fill in the blanks below with **gh**. Then pronounce the words in the sentences.*

1. The patient thou*gh*t that she gave the doctor her ri*gh*t hei*gh*t and wei*gh*t.

2. The strong li____t was bri____t at ni____t.

3. The hi____ school principal cau____t two boys in the hall. He brou____t them to the office because they fou____t.

4. They thou____t that they bou____t the ri____t kind of li____t beer for the picnic.

WHAT KIND OF CAR ARE YOU LOOKING FOR?

COMPETENCIES	• Reading Road Signs
	• Requesting Information about the Price and Condition of a Car
	• Reading Newspaper Car Ads
GRAMMAR	• How long does *it take*?
VOCABULARY	• Common Road Signs
	• Parts of a Car
WORD BUILDING	• The Suffix *-ward*

LISTEN

Rita Landry and David Fernandez are talking about Rita's driving test.

Rita: I'm nervous. I'm going to take my driving test today.
David: How long did it take you to learn to drive?
Rita: It took me a few months.
David: Are you ready for the tests?
Rita: I think so.
David: What do you have to do?
Rita: I have to pass a vision test, a driving test, and a test on traffic rules of the road.
David: How long will the tests take?
Rita: I think they'll take about an hour.
David: Where do you take the tests?
Rita: At the Department of Motor Vehicles.
David: Where's that?
Rita: On the corner of Fourth and A Streets. It takes only a few minutes to get there from here.
David: Do you know all the rules?
Rita: I think so. I studied them in a driver's manual.
David: What about the road signs? Do you understand them?
Rita: Test me!

UNDERSTAND   *Circle True, False, or We don't know.*

1. It took Rita about sixty days to learn to drive a car.	True	False	We don't know.
2. Rita is ready to take the test.	True	False	We don't know.
3. Rita will pass the test.	True	False	We don't know.
4. There are three kinds of tests.	True	False	We don't know.
5. The Department of Motor Vehicles isn't far.	True	False	We don't know.

GRAMMAR   *it takes*

- We use the expression **it takes** to describe the amount of time we need to do an action or to go a distance.
- We can use an indirect object after the expression.

EXAMPLES			*Time*	
It	**took**	me	**a few months**	to learn to drive.
It'll	**take**		**about an hour**	to take the test.
It only	**takes**		**a few minutes**	to go there.

READ   *Make logical complete sentences with the words in the box.*

It	takes took will take	me him her us them	a short time a few minutes an hour five days all day half an hour a long time	to drive to New York. to get here. to go to work. to do the job. to take the test. to learn English. to eat dinner.

PAIR PRACTICE   *Talk with another student about the actions below. Use the present tense.*

Student 1: How long does it take to ....?
Student 2: It takes .... to ....

1. get to school
2. do the homework in this class
3. learn a language
4. learn English well
5. fly to New York from here
6. go home by bus
7. learn to drive
8. walk home from here
9. ....

PAIR PRACTICE   *Use the past tense.*

Student 1: How long did it take you to ....?
Student 2: It took me .... to ....

1. get ready this morning
2. come to this country
3. make breakfast this morning
4. make dinner last night
5. find an apartment
6. come to school
7. learn English
8. clean your house last week
9. do your food shopping last week
10. ....

READ

Here are some road signs from the driver's manual.

1. No left turn

2. Two-way traffic

3. Railroad crossing

4. No U turns

5. Yield

6. Merging traffic

7. Crossroad

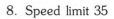

8. Speed limit 35

9. Stop

10. One way

11. Do not enter

12. School

13. Signal ahead

14. Side road

15. Fewer lanes ahead   16. Left turn

READ

WRITE   *Match the signs and the meanings.* * *Write the letters of the meanings in the spaces under the signs.*

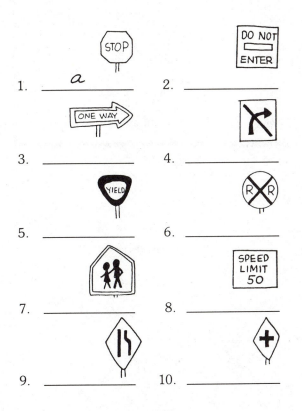

1. _____ *a* _____
2. _____
3. _____
4. _____
5. _____
6. _____
7. _____
8. _____
9. _____
10. _____

a.   This sign means "stop."

b.   This sign means that you can drive in only one direction.

c.   This sign means that you cannot drive on this street.

d.   This sign means that you must let other cars go first.

e.   This sign means that you cannot turn right.

f.   This sign means that there are railroad tracks ahead.

g.   This sign means that there's an intersection ahead.

h.   This sign means that there's a school crossing ahead.

i.   This sign means that you cannot drive over 50 miles per hour.

j.   This sign means that two lanes become one lane.

---

* See the end of this chapter for more words and phrases used on road signs.

READ

WHAT DO THE COLORS AND SHAPES OF THE SIGNS MEAN?

OH, THAT'S EASY.

SHAPE		MEANING
octagon		stop
triangle		yield
circle		railroad crossing
diamond		warning
square		traffic
		no passing
		school

COLOR	MEANING
red	danger, stop
orange	construction
yellow	general warning
green	direction and distance
blue	service
white	traffic rules
brown	public recreation areas
black	night speed limit

PAIR PRACTICE   *Talk with another student about road signs. Use the colors above.*

Student 1: What does .... mean?
Student 2: It means ....

WHAT DOES RED MEAN?

IT MEANS DANGER.

PAIR PRACTICE   *Point to the shapes.*

Student 1: What does this shape mean?
Student 2: It means ....

IT MEANS STOP.

WHAT DOES THIS SHAPE MEAN?

WRITE   *Fill in the spaces below with the words in the box. Use the map.*

one way	left	right	25	railroad crossing
yield	stopped	turned	2nd and A	do not enter

It's the following day. Rita is telling David about her driving test.

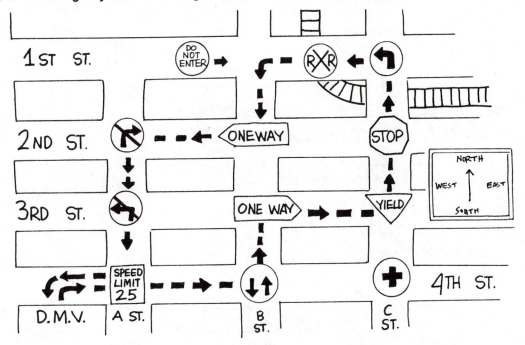

Rita: I passed my driving test. I did very well. Let me tell you all about it. We
began at the Department of Motor Vehicles at the corner of 4th and A
Streets. The sign at that corner said that the speed limit was (1)___*25*___
mph. I drove east to 4th and B Streets and turned (2)_____. I went
one block and turned (3)_____ on 3rd Street. I drove one block. I saw
a sign at the corner of 3rd and C Streets. It said (4)_____, so I drove
slowly. Then, I (5)_____ north. I (6)_____ at the corner of 2nd
and C Streets. After I turned west, I crossed a (7)_____ _____. I
drove to 1st and B Streets. I saw a sign there. It said (8)_____, so I
didn't continue on 1st Street. I turned south and went one block and turned
west on 2nd Street because it's a (9)_____ _____ street. I drove
one block, and then turned south at (10)_____ Streets. I drove past 3rd
Street and arrived back at the Department of Motor Vehicles.

READ

David and Rita are talking about cars.

Rita: I have my license. Now I want to buy a car.
David: What kind of car do you want?
Rita: I want a nice, small, beautiful, new, inexpensive car.
And it has to get good mileage!
David: I'm sorry, but nobody has that kind of car.
Do you want a domestic or foreign car?
Rita: It doesn't matter.
David: What kind of equipment do you want on the car?
Rita: Look at this. I made a list of equipment.

---

two doors
automatic transmission
power brakes
stereo and AM-FM radio
power steering
air conditioning
six cylinders
nice interior
good gas mileage
good general condition

UNDERSTAND   *Circle **True**, **False**, or **We don't know**.*

1. Rita needs a car.	True	False	We don't know.
2. Rita wants to buy a foreign car.	True	False	We don't know.
3. Rita wants a car with power brakes.	True	False	We don't know.
4. She doesn't want power steering.	True	False	We don't know.

PAIR PRACTICE   *Talk with another student. Use Rita's list above.*

Student 1: What kind of equipment does Rita want on the car?
Student 2: She wants ....

READ   *Use your dictionaries.*

HATCHBACK power brakes 4 cylinders good gas mileage must sell $4000 call 231-0952	**CONVERTIBLE** excellent condition AM/FM radio runs well $5995 call after 6 p.m. 494-9237
SEDAN 4 doors air conditioning automatic transmission low mileage $6000 943-5867	**VAN** good condition financing available nice interior, clean call weekends 695-2581
SPORTS CAR power steering standard transmission stereo great deal $5500 call 812-5493	**PICKUP TRUCK** needs work rebuilt engine new tires best offer 369-0842
STATION WAGON 40,000 miles excellent condition one owner private party telephone 653-0912	**RECREATION VEHICLE** good shape mint condition 3 years old make offer 399-4339

HERE ARE SOME NEWSPAPER ADS.

PAIR PRACTICE   *Talk with another student. Use the ads above.*

Student 1: What kind of equipment does the .... have?
Student 2: It has ....

IT HAS AN AM/FM RADIO.

WHAT KIND OF EQUIPMENT DOES THE CONVERTIBLE HAVE?

PAIR PRACTICE   *Use the ads above.*

Student 1: Does the ....?
Student 2: Yes, it does. / No, it doesn't.

YES, IT DOES.

DOES THE PICKUP TRUCK NEED WORK?

PAIR PRACTICE   *Use the ads above.*

Student 1: Is the ....?
Student 2: Yes, it is. / No, it isn't.

IS THE STATION WAGON IN GOOD CONDITION?

YES, IT IS.

READ

Rita is calling about the sports car.

Rita: Hello, do you have a car for sale?
Man: Yes, I do.
Rita: What kind of car is it?
Man: It's a five-year-old domestic car.
Rita: What color is the car?
Man: Beige.
Rita: What's the condition of the car?
Man: It's in excellent condition.
Rita: How much are you asking for it?
Man: $5500.
Rita: When can I see it?
Man: Anytime. I'll be home all day. My address is 211 Olympic Drive.
Rita: Good. I'll be there soon.

UNDERSTAND   *Circle **True**, **False**, or **We don't know**.*

1. "What are you asking?" means "How much does it cost?"	True	False	We don't know.
2. The car costs $5500.	True	False	We don't know.
3. Rita knows the man's address.	True	False	We don't know.

PAIR PRACTICE   *Talk with another student. Use the signs below.*

Student 1: What's the price and condition of the ....?
Student 2: It's .... and it's in ....

READ   *Parts of a car.*

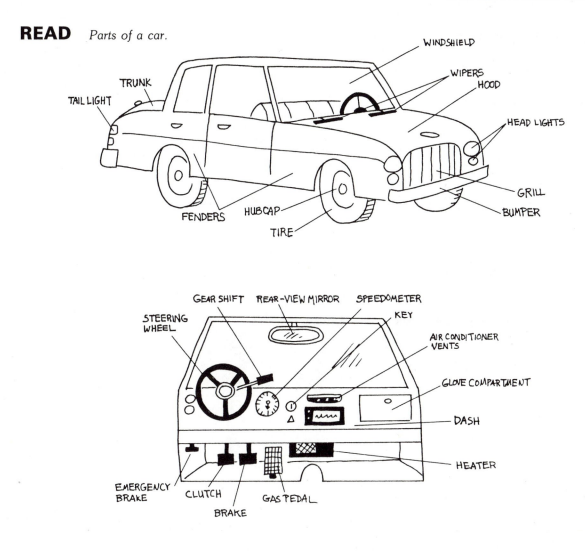

PAIR PRACTICE   *Talk about the parts of a car. Use the prepositions in the box to describe where they are located.*

on the outside of	in the front of	on the side of
on the inside of	in the back of	at the corners of

Student 1: Where is/are ....?
Student 2: It's/They're ....

WRITE   *Help Rita ask about the car. The answers will help you figure out the questions.*

Rita is looking at the sports car.

Rita: *Do you have a car for sale* ?

Man: Yes, I have a car for sale.

Rita: _____ ?

Man: The tires are in very good condition.

Rita: _____ ?

Man: Yes, it has power brakes and power steering, too.

Rita: _____ ?

Man: 30,000 miles.

Rita: _____ ?

Man: I'm asking $5500 for this car.

Rita: _____ ?

Man: OK. You can have the car for $5000.

DICTATION   *Cover the sentences under each line. Write the dictation on the line as your teacher reads it to you. Then uncover the sentences and correct your writing.*

Dear Mom and Dad,

1. _____
   I took my driving test yesterday and passed.

2. _____
   It only took me a few months to learn to drive.

3. _____
   I bought a used sports car, but it's in very good condition.

4. _____
   It has a radio, power brakes, and standard transmission.

5. _____
   I'll write you more about my new car later.

   Love, Rita

PAIR PRACTICE

Fold the page down the middle. Look only at your side. Do the exercise orally.

Student 1	**Student 2**

Don't show your picture to your partner. Tell him/her where the signs are in your picture and what is on the sign. Your partner will write that information in his or her picture. Compare both pictures only after your partner fills in all the information.

Don't look at your partner's picture. Fill in the signs. Your partner will tell you where and what to write in the signs.

Now fill in your signs with the information from your partner.

Now tell your partner where the signs are in your picture and what is on the signs.

FOLD HERE

WORD BUILDING   The Suffix *-ward*

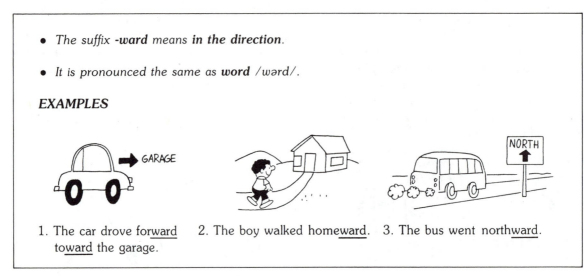

- *The suffix **-ward** means **in the direction**.*

- *It is pronounced the same as **word** /wərd/.*

EXAMPLES

1. The car drove for<u>ward</u> to<u>ward</u> the garage.

2. The boy walked home<u>ward</u>.

3. The bus went north<u>ward</u>.

WRITE   *Fill in the crossword puzzle with the **opposites** of the words on the left.*

DOWN

1. westward
3. inward
4. downward
6. eastward
7. outward

ACROSS

2. backward
5. northward
8. upward
9. inward

Crossword:
1. (down) E A S T W A R D

OTHER WORDS AND PHRASES USED IN ROAD SIGNS

Regulatory Signs

END 25 MILE ZONE
NO STOPPING ANY TIME
TRUCK ROUTE
NO PED CROSSING
LEFT TURN ON LEFT ARROW ONLY
TURNOUT 1/4 MILE
COMMERCIAL VEHICLES PROHIBITED
MAXIMUM SPEED LIMIT 55 MILES
LOAD LIMIT 10 TONS
NO PARKING ANY TIME
SPEED CHECKED BY RADAR
$500 FINE FOR LITTERING
SLOWER TRAFFIC USE TURNOUTS
NO BICYCLES
TWO-LANE TRAFFIC AHEAD
DO NOT PASS
SLOWER TRAFFIC KEEP RIGHT
U TURN OK
AFTER STOP RIGHT TURN PERMITTED ON RED
NO RIGHT TURN
NO FISHING FROM BRIDGE
PARK OFF PAVEMENT
TOW AWAY ZONE
EMERGENCY PARKING ONLY
PARK PARALLEL
NO LEFT TURN 4 P.M. TO 6 P.M.
PASSING LANE AHEAD
BEGIN FREEWAY
PASS WITH CARE
USE CROSSWALK
3-WAY SIGNAL
SIGNALS SET FOR 23 MPH
RIGHT LANE MUST TURN RIGHT
15 MPH ON BRIDGE FOR VEHICLES OVER 10 TONS
RIGHT TURN ONLY
LEFT TURN ONLY
NO TURNS
LEFT TURN LANE
PEDESTRIANS, BICYCLES, MOTOR DRIVEN
   CYCLES PROHIBITED
BUSES AND CAR POOLS ONLY

Guide Signs

HISTORICAL LANDMARK
ELEVATION 3000 FT
GAS FOOD LODGING
NEXT SERVICES 22 MILES
REST AREA

Warning Signs

ROAD NARROWS
SOFT SHOULDER
PAVEMENT ENDS
NARROW BRIDGE
RANGE CATTLE
END
TUNNEL
DIVIDED ROAD
PED XING
CROSS TRAFFIC AHEAD
NARROW SUBWAY
NO OUTLET
SLIPPERY WHEN WET
THRU TRAFFIC MERGE LEFT
ISLANDS
SLOW
LANE ENDS MERGE LEFT
HILL
DIP
DRIFTING SAND
FLOODED
EXIT 30 M.P.H.
SLIDE AREA
RAMP 30 M.P.H.
BIKE XING
ICY NEXT 4 MILES
BRIDLE PATH
SCHOOL BUS STOP 400 FT
BUMP
FALLING ROCKS
SLOW TRUCKS
ROUGH ROAD
LOW CLEARANCE 12 FT 6 IN
NOT A THROUGH STREET
SCHOOL
ONE-LANE BRIDGE
DEER AREA

Construction Signs

DETOUR AHEAD
LOOSE GRAVEL
OPEN TRENCH
FLAGMAN AHEAD
SLIDE AREA
ROAD WORK AHEAD
ROAD CLOSED TO THRU TRAFFIC
BRIDGE OUT
ROAD CLOSED
PREPARE TO STOP

15

DO YOU WORK HARD OR HARDLY WORK?

COMPETENCIES	• Describing How People Work
GRAMMAR	• Adjectives and Adverbs
	• Regular and Irregular Forms of Adverbs
VOCABULARY	• Common Adjectives and Adverbs
	• Important Safety Signs
	• *hardly*
WORD BUILDING	• The Suffixes *-tion* and *-sion*
SPELLING	• Rules for Adding *-ly* to Words

LISTEN

James Fuller and Roy Barns are talking in the adult school hall.

  Roy: Hi, James. How's it going?

 James: Not bad. How about you?

  Roy: OK. It's almost the end of the semester, and I have to give a final test. There
     are a lot of nervous students in my ESL class. How are your students?

 James: Busy. Their final is a woodshop project. They're doing it right now. Come
     on, I'll show you.

  Roy: How are they working?

 James: They're working steadily.

  Roy: I can see that.

 James: There's David Fernandez. He's a quick and accurate worker.

  Roy: Oh, yes, David. He was in my class last year.

 James: And there's Paul Green. He works a little slowly, but he's a very careful
     worker. He always does everything correctly.
     There's Joanne Yates. She's an attentive and safe student. And next to her,
     there's Roberto Monte. He left his project temporarily because he's helping a
     slow student. Roberto explains directions very clearly.
     There's only one problem.

  Roy: What's that?

 James: The machines run too noisily.

UNDERSTAND *Circle True, False, or We don't know.*

1. "How's it going?" means "How are you?"	True	False	We don't know.
2. Mr. Fuller has a lot of nervous students.	True	False	We don't know.
3. All the students are working nicely.	True	False	We don't know.
4. Roberto finished his project.	True	False	We don't know.
5. The machines don't run very quietly.	True	False	We don't know.

GRAMMAR   Adjectives and Regular Adverbs

- *Adjectives modify nouns and precede them.*
- *Adjectives generally appear in answers to questions with **What kind of ...?***
- *Adverbs modify verbs and usually follow them.*
- *Many common adverbs are formed by adding the suffix **-ly**.*
- *Adverbs generally appear in answers to questions with **How ...?***

EXAMPLES

	Adjectives	Nouns	
There are a lot of	nervous	students	in my class.
David's an	accurate	worker.	
David's a	quick	worker.	
Paul Green's a	careful	worker.	
Joanne Yates is an	attentive	student.	
Joanne's a	safe	student.	

	Verbs		Adverbs
They	're working		steadily.
Paul	does	everything	correctly.
Roberto	left	his project	temporarily.
He	explains	directions	clearly.
The machines	run		noisily.
The students	are working		nicely.

READ   *Make logical complete sentences with the words in the boxes.*

David			quick	person.
Paul	's	a	accurate	machine.
Joanne	isn't		noisy	worker.
Roberto		an	careful	man.
It			attentive	woman.

David	work on		carefully.
Paul	works on	directions	clearly.
Joanne	explain	his/her project	nicely.
Roberto	explains	his/her work	correctly.
The students	do	everything	steadily.
I	does		slowly.

PAIR PRACTICE   *Talk with another student. Supply your own verbs.*

Student 1: How does ....?
Student 2: He/She/It ....ly.

1. David's a quick worker.

2. Joanne's an attentive student.

3. Paul's a careful student.

4. Roberto's a clear speaker.

5. This is a steady worker.

6. It's a noisy machine.

PAIR PRACTICE   *Use the phrases below.*

Student 1: What kind of .... is ....?
Student 2: He/She/It is a ....

1. The machine works noisily.

2. Sami studies nervously.

3. This student is working steadily.

4. Roy's listening calmly.

5. Roberto speaks clearly.

6. Paul's working correctly.

7. Joanne works safely.

8. David works accurately.

SPELLING   Rules for Adding *-ly* to Words

- *Most adverbs are formed by simply adding* **-ly**.

EXAMPLES   quick → quick<u>ly</u>   attentive → attentive<u>ly</u>
                slow → slow<u>ly</u>   correct → correct<u>ly</u>

- *The letter* **y** *changes to* **i** *before adding* **-ly**.

EXAMPLES   busy → busi<u>ly</u>   temporary → temporari<u>ly</u>
                noisy → noisi<u>ly</u>   steady → steadi<u>ly</u>

- *When a word ends in* **le**, *drop the* **e**, *and simply add* **y**. *The letter* **e** *is no longer pronounced*.

EXAMPLES   comfortable → comfortab<u>ly</u>
                terrible → terrib<u>ly</u>

- ***Do not*** *drop a final* **l** *when adding* **-ly**.

EXAMPLES   careful → carefu<u>lly</u>
                normal → norma<u>lly</u>

WRITE   *Fill in the spaces with the opposite of the adverb in the question. Make sure that you spell the adverb correctly.*

1. Do you have any careless students?	All my students work *Carefully*.
2. Do you have any slow students?	No, they all work _____.
3. Are there any inaccurate students?	No, they all work _____.
4. Are there any inattentive students?	No, they listen _____.
5. Do any students work incorrectly?	No, they work _____.
6. Do they work noisily?	No, they work _____.
7. Do they work nervously?	No, everybody works _____.
8. Do the machines run quietly?	No, they run too _____.

READ

Roy Barns and James Fuller are talking about Raymond Monte.

IS RAYMOND A GOOD, HARD WORKER?

HE SURE IS. HE WORKS HARD, FAST, AND WELL. HE HARDLY EVER STOPS.

GRAMMAR   Irregular Adverbs

- *Unlike most adverbs, **well**, **fast**, and **hard** do not end in **-ly**.*

EXAMPLES   **How**   does Raymond work?   He works   **hard.**

- *Don't confuse **hard** with **hardly**.*

   1. **Hardly** is an adverb of manner.
   2. **Hardly** is often used with **ever**.
   3. **Hardly** answers the question **How often ...?** It means **almost never**.

EXAMPLES

| **How often** | does he stop? | He | **hardly** | stops. |
| **How often** | do you eat out? | We | **hardly ever** | eat out. |

READ   *Make logical complete sentences with the words in the boxes.*

Raymond	works	
I	work	well.
We	study	hard.
The students	studies	fast.
She	learn	
	learns	

| Do you | study play work listen | hard, | or | do you | hardly | study? play? work? listen? |

CHALLENGE   *Answer the questions you made with the words in the box above.*

PAIR PRACTICE   *Talk about the pictures below. Use the words **well**, **hard**, or **fast** in the answers.*

Student 1: How should a .... work?
Student 2: He/She/It .... should work ....

1. construction worker
2. typist
3. surgeon
4. machine

5. miner
6. assembly line worker
7. pilot
8. athlete

9. nurse
10. dentist
11. mail carrier
12. student

PAIR PRACTICE   *Talk about the activities below. Use **often** or **hardly ever** in the answers.*

Student 1: How often do you ....?
Student 2: .... often/hardly ever ....

1. go to a restaurant
2. go to the movies
3. spend a lot of money on clothes
4. buy expensive presents
5. get gifts

6. take long trips
7. go shopping at night
8. watch T.V. in the morning
9. get a raise
10. ....

CHALLENGE   *Tell what the signs in the picture mean.*

CHALLENGE   *How many dangerous situations can you identify in the picture above? List them below.*

1. _____
2. _____
3. _____
4. _____
5. _____
6. _____
7. _____
8. _____
9. _____
10. _____
11. _____
12. _____

GROUP ACTIVITY   *Find the students in your class with the following qualities. Then write their names in the spaces below.*

HOW WELL DO YOU KNOW YOUR CLASSMATES?

1. _____
   is a good learner.

2. _____
   speaks well.

3. _____
   writes well.

4. _____
   reads correctly.

5. _____
   is a steady worker.

6. _____
   does all the homework accurately.

7. _____
   reads fast.

8. _____
   works quietly.

9. _____
   listens attentively.

10. _____
    is a calm person.

11. _____
    speaks clearly.

12. _____
    teaches well.

WORD BUILDING   **The Suffixes *-tion* and *-sion***

- *We usually pronounce the suffix **-tion** as /sh-n/ or /ch-n/.*
- *We always use **-tion** after the letter **a**.*
- *We pronounce **-sion** as /sh-n/, /zh-n/, and /ch-n/ (as in **question**).*
- *We use **-tion** more than **-sion**.*

EXAMPLES

1. vision

2. question

3. nation

4. direction

5. construction

6. profession

7. station

8. operation

WRITE   *Fill in the spaces with **-tion** or **-sion**, then pronounce the sentences.*

1. When I studied mathematics, we learned addi_*tion*_, subtrac_____, multiplica_____, and divi_____.

2. How are my pronuncia_____ and intona_____ when I ask ques_____s?

3. Joanne got some direc_____s at the informa_____ sec_____ of the bus sta_____.

4. What are the direc_____ and opera_____ of the revolu_____ in that na_____?

5. There are a lot of excep_____s and varia_____s in English spelling.

16

MY ENGLISH IS BETTER EVERY DAY

- Review Chapter
- Final Test

LISTEN

It's breaktime at school. A few students are talking.

Joanne: Did you hear?
  Rita: No, what?
Joanne: David Fernandez lost his job.
  Rita: No kidding! What happened?
Joanne: His company laid him off.
  Rita: Why?
Joanne: The economy!

UNDERSTAND   *Circle True, False, or We don't know.*

1. "A few" means "over 100."   True   False   We don't know.
2. David Fernandez has a job.   True   False   We don't know.
3. "No kidding!" means "Really?"   True   False   We don't know.
4. David lost his job because he doesn't work hard.   True   False   We don't know.

WRITE   *Rewrite the verbs under the lines in the past tense.*

Here comes David.

Joanne: Hi, David. How's it going?

  David: Not too well. I __*lost*__ my job.
                        lose

Joanne: What _____?
                happen

  David: I _____ this morning, and _____ everything as usual. When I
           get up \   **do**

           _____ at work, I _____ a pink piece of paper on my time
            arrive   **find**

           card. It _____ to see the personnel manager, so I _____ to
                      say   **go**

           the office and spoke to her. She _____ me that business
                                              tell

           _____ bad and that they _____ lay off fifty percent of the
              is   **have to**

           work force. Now I have to find a new job.

READ

WRITE *Fill in an application for a job.*

APPLICATION

(please print)

Name: Mr./Mrs./Ms./Miss (circle one)

_____

        Last   First   Middle

Address: _____

          Street Number   Street   Apartment
                                                            Number

City: _____ State: _____ Zip Code: _____

Telephone Number: _____

                        Home   Work or School

Place of Birth: _____ Sex: (Check one)

                    City   Country   Male   ☐
                                                                 Female   ☐

Date of
Birth: _____/_____/_____   Age: _____
        Month   Date   Year

Color of Hair: _____   Color of Eyes: _____

Marital Status: (Underline one)   Married / Single / Divorced / Separated / Widowed

Are you a citizen of this country? (circle one)   YES   NO

What is your present occupation? _____

Today's Date: _____   Signature: _____

CHALLENGE *Which questions in the questionnaire are illegal?*

WRITE   *Fold this page down the middle. Do this exercise with a partner. Each of you will select a side. Tell your partner what messages there are on your bulletin board, and your partner will write them on his or her bulletin board. Then reverse roles. Compare your papers only after you both finish.*

READ

The students are back in class after the break.

Joanne: It's almost the weekend. We have two days off.
Rita: Maybe, but I have to do my housework. What are you going to do?
Joanne: I'm going to a party.

PAIR PRACTICE

*Talk with another student. Use expressions with **do** and the activities below in the answers.*

Student 1: What do you have to do tomorrow?
Student 2: I have to ....

1. some housework   2. the cooking   3. the dishes   4. the shopping

5. the laundry   6. the ironing   7. the vacuuming   8. the dusting

PAIR PRACTICE

*Use expressions with **get** and the phrases below in the answers.*

Student 1: What are you going to do?
Student 2: I'm going to get ....

1. a haircut   2. up late   3. the mail   4. a check

5. new clothes   6. ready for the party   7. a taxi   8. there on time

READ

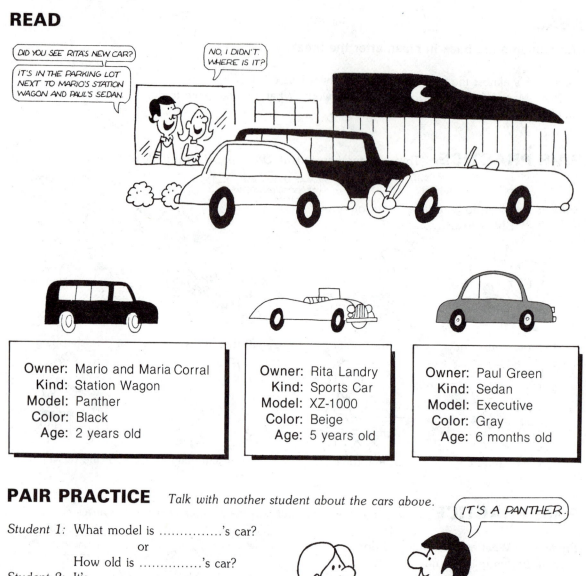

Owner: Mario and Maria Corral
Kind: Station Wagon
Model: Panther
Color: Black
Age: 2 years old

Owner: Rita Landry
Kind: Sports Car
Model: XZ-1000
Color: Beige
Age: 5 years old

Owner: Paul Green
Kind: Sedan
Model: Executive
Color: Gray
Age: 6 months old

PAIR PRACTICE   *Talk with another student about the cars above.*

Student 1:   What model is ....'s car?
                             or
               How old is ....'s car?
Student 2:   It's ....

PAIR PRACTICE   *Talk about the cars above.*

Student 1:   Whose car is ....?
Student 2:   ....'s car is.

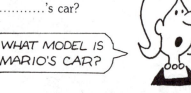

READ

  Rita: How are you getting home?

David: I'm walking.

  Rita: I have a car. Do you want a ride?

David: Oh, "si." I mean, yes. How do you say "yes" in French?

  Rita: "Oui." We pronounce it /wē/.

UNDERSTAND   *Circle* **True**, **False**, *or* **We don't know**.

1. David has a car.	True	False	We don't know.
2. Rita speaks French.	True	False	We don't know.
3. David will walk home tonight.	True	False	We don't know.

PAIR PRACTICE   *Ask about the words below. Supply the answers.*

Student 1: How do you say "................" in your language?

Student 2: We say "................"

1. yes
2. no
3. hello
4. good-bye
5. please

6. thank you
7. How are you?
8. man
9. woman
10. ....

PAIR PRACTICE   *Review the letters of the alphabet before doing this exercise.*

Student 1: How do you spell "................"?

Student 2: "................"

Student 1: How do you pronounce it?

Student 2: We pronounce it /................/.

1. your first name
2. your last name
3 your middle name (if you have one)
4. the name of your street
5. the name of your city or town

6. the name of your state
7. the name of your country
8. the name of your profession
9. the month of your birth
10. the ....

READ

David Fernandez and Mr. Barns are talking in the hall in front of the ESL classroom. The students are taking their final exam.

David: How are you, Mr. Barns?

Roy: Pretty good. How are you doing?

David: Not so good. I lost my job today.

Roy: I'm sorry to hear that.

David: How are your students doing?

Roy: They're very nervous about their final test.

David: I remember that you gave our class a hard final last year. I really learned a lot when I was in your class.

Roy: Thanks for the compliment.

David: Now I can speak English good. I'll need it to find a job.

Roy: If you speak English "good," you don't speak English "well."

David: Oh, sorry! But my English is improving. Don't you think so?

Roy: Yes, I do. Your English is better every day!

UNDERSTAND   *Circle True, False, or We don't know.*

1. David was in Mr. Barns' class last year.	True	False	We don't know.
2. David's English isn't improving.	True	False	We don't know.
3. David doesn't need English to find a job.	True	False	We don't know.
4. Your English is better every day.	True	False	We don't know.

FINAL TEST   *Circle the correct answers.*

1. How _____ do you come to school?
   a. sometimes   c. never
   b. often   d. seldom

2. David doesn't have a job; he's _____.
   a. temporary   c. employed
   b. permanent   d. unemployed

3. When people are sick, they don't feel very
   _____.
   a. hard   c. hardly
   b. weak   d. well

4. David _____ get a job.
   a. has   c. have
   b. has to   d. have to

5. How's the weather outside? Is it _____?
   a. raining   c. expensive
   b. working   d. cheap

6. Joanne doesn't _____ work on Sunday.
   a. has   c. have
   b. has to   d. have to

7. What kind of car does Joanne _____?
   a. has   c. have
   b. has to   d. have to

8. David will call the company _____ ask
   about a job.
   a. for   c. in
   b. too   d. in order to

9. _____ David find a good job?
   a. Going   c. Want
   b. Will   d. Need

10. The company _____ close.
    a. no   c. no will
    b. not   d. won't

11. Will that be all? _____.
    a. Please, yes.   c. Yes, I will.
    b. Yes, that's all.   d. Thank you.

12. When _____ on our next picnic?
    a. we going   c. are we going
    b. are going   d. we are going

13. We're _____ to have the picnic as usual.
    a. go   c. go to
    b. going to   d. going

14. Will you take a walk with me? No, not now.
    Maybe later. I _____ to rest now.
    a. want   c. won't
    b. will   d. going to

15. Many students _____ at the picnic.
    a. was   c. were
    b. where   d. wear

16. How _____ the weather yesterday?
    a. was   c. were
    b. where   d. wear

17. What kind _____ was there?
    a. of food   c. foods
    b. off food   d. food

18. This test isn't very _____; it's easy.
    a. complicated   c. really
    b. understand   d. directions

19. Please don't _____ that box.
    a. spill   c. fall
    b. drop   d. fell

20. Rita _____ to buy a new car.
    a. decide   c. will
    b. decided   d. want

21. _____ car did Sami paint?
    a. How much   c. Whose
    b. Who   d. How

22. When _____ you arrive here?
    a. are   c. was
    b. did   d. were

23. Nancy's sister _____ her two theater tickets in New York.
    a. buy
    b. will buys
    c. buyed
    d. bought

24. Can I ask you a few questions? Yes, _____.
    a. I can
    b. you can
    c. can
    d. can't

25. Do you have any relatives here? Yes, _____.
    a. I did
    b. I was
    c. I does
    d. I do

26. Please _____ the T.V. before you look inside it.
    a. place
    b. turn
    c. unplug
    d. plug

27. Turn _____ the light; I can't see.
    a. of
    b. on
    c. in
    d. away

28. All the members of the family _____ the shopping.
    a. do
    b. does
    c. make
    d. makes

29. Please don't _____ any mistakes.
    a. do
    b. does
    c. make
    d. makes

30. James _____ some new shoes at the store a few months ago.
    a. got
    b. get
    c. buy
    d. getted

31. Carmen _____ the bus after a long ride home.
    a. go off
    b. got off
    c. get off
    d. get on

32. She looked _____ to see the airplane.
    a. on
    b. up
    c. at
    d. to

33. Please throw the garbage _____.
    a. out
    b. way
    c. off
    d. why

34. Please take _____ your coat.
    a. on
    b. up
    c. of
    d. off

35. Please get me a _____ milk.
    a. bottle
    b. of bottle
    c. bottles
    d. bottle of

36. You can find the milk in _____ 10.
    a. Information
    b. Section
    c. Directory
    d. Piece

37. There are 16 ounces in a _____.
    a. pint
    b. pound
    c. quart
    d. kilo

38. I _____ to make an appointment.
    a. would
    b. will
    c. 'd like
    d. likes

39. Where _____ it hurt?
    a. do
    b. does
    c. is
    d. was

40. I have _____ in my left hand.
    a. some weak
    b. some hurt
    c. some pain
    d. weak

41. People can get immediate help in an _____ room.
    a. operating
    b. emergency
    c. waiting
    d. lab

42. I _____ that David lost his job.
    a. was hear
    b. heared
    c. heard
    d. hear

43. What did the doctor _____ to Betty?
    a. said
    b. tell
    c. told
    d. say

44. He _____ her that she had a little arthritis.
    a. said
    b. tell
    c. told
    d. say

45. Please turn left at that "one way" _____.
    a. sign
    b. signs
    c. picture
    d. directions

46. What kind of _____ does Rita's car have?
    a. standard   c. equipment
    b. cylinders   d. conditions

47. Her car is in excellent _____.
    a. standard   c. brakes
    b. condition   d. power

48. The woodshop students work very _____.
    a. careful   c. careless
    b. carefully   d. quick

49. The students are _____ workers.
    a. careful   c. carelessly
    b. carefully   d. quickly

50. If you speak English "good," you don't speak English _____.
    a. will   c. good
    b. very   d. well

CHALLENGE   *After you correct the test, calculate your grade below.*

1. Write the number of *correct* answers in the box below.

    CORRECT ANSWERS ⟶

2. Multiply the number of correct answers by 2.

    CORRECT ANSWER [   ] x 2 = [   ]

3. Find your letter grade below.

    90% to 100% = A   (excellent)
    75% to 89% = B   (above average)
    60% to 74% = C   (average)
    45% to 59% = D   (below average)
     0% to 44% = F   (failure)

4. Write your final grade in the box below.

    MY FINAL GRADE: [   ]

WORD LIST